Spirituality and Community

Diversity in Lesbian & Gay Experience

Gay Men's Issues in Religious Studies Series,
Volume 5

Proceedings
of the
Gay Men's Issues in Religion Group
of the
American Academy of Religion,
San Francisco, CA

Fall 1992

Edited by
J. Michael Clark
&
Michael L. Stemmeler

Las Colinas
Monument Press
1994

BL
65
.H64
S65
1994

Published by
Monument Press
Las Colinas, Texas

Copyright 1994, Monument Press

Library of Congress Cataloging-in-Publication Data

Spirituality and community : diversity in lesbian and gay experience ;
   essays / by Roger J. Corless . . . [et al.] ; edited by J. Michael
   Clark & Michael L. Stemmeler.
          p. cm. -- (Gay men's issues in religious studies series ; v.
5)
   "Proceedings of the Gay Men's Issues in Religion Group of the
American Academy of Religion, San Francisco, CA, Fall 1992."
   Includes bibliographical references.
   ISBN 0-930383-43-5 (pbk.) : $25.00
   1. Homosexuality--Religious aspects--Congresses. 2. Gay men-
-Religious life--Congresses. 3. Lesbians--Religious life-
-Congresses. I. Corless, Roger. II. Clark, J. Michael (John
Michael), 1953-   . III. Stemmeler, Michael L., 1955-   .
IV. American Academy of Religion. Gay Men's Issues in Religion
Group. V. Series.
BL65.H64S65 1994
291.4'08'664--dc20   94-4137
                                                             CIP

Gay Men's Issues in Religious Studies Series

under the general editorship of

J. Michael Clark & Michael L. Stemmeler

Forthcoming

in the

Gay Men's Issues
in
Religious Studies Series:

Volume 6

Proceedings
of the
Gay Men's Issues in Religion Group
of the
American Academy of Religion
Washington, D.C.
Fall 1993

Topics will include:

Identity, (Bio)Diversity, and Sexuality
and
Homophobia in the Profession

* * *

Table of Contents

- VI -

Part B. **Families and Coalitions: Lesbians and Gay Men Creating New Patterns of Community**

Michael L. Stemmeler

Preface

The present volume on *Spirituality and Community: Diversity in Lesbian & Gay Experience* marks the fifth volume of the Gay Men's Issues in Religious Studies Series. It bears the fruit of two program sessions conducted by the Gay Men's Issues in Religion Group at the 1992 annual meeting of the American Academy of Religion in San Francisco.

Part A: *Gay Spirituality, AIDS, and Ecclesiology* presents the revised versions of the papers that were delivered in the Gay Men's Issues in Religion Group's own program session. Part B: *Families and Coalitions: Lesbians and Gay Men Creating New Patterns of Community* advances the edited contributions to the first jointly sponsored session of the Gay Men's and the Lesbian/Feminist Issues in Religion Groups.

Under the headline *Gay Spirituality, AIDS, and Ecclesiology* Susan Henking, Richard Hardy, Roger Corless, and Dan Spencer investigate the meanings of life and spirituality and the possibility for the development of an ecclesiology for Gay people at a time when they are existentially challenged by AIDS. Since the early '80s AIDS has thrown its shadow over all theologizing and philosophizing. No Gay theory and practice that claim to be authentic and want to be taken seriously can step behind AIDS and pretend it had not happened.

Susan Henking provides a detailed analysis of AIDS–related memoirs and Richard Hardy introduces his view of persons living with AIDS as prophets of an authentic spirituality. Roger Corless contributes a serious treatise on the possibility of

Gay male spirituality in mainstream religions beyond mere acceptance, an essay which incidentally never loses its humorous subtone. Dan Spencer attempts first to be ecclesiologically iconoclastic and then dares the reconstruction of an ecclesial community and theory which can, no, which has to be experienced as liberating by Lesbians and Gay men. All essays are powerful and timely contributions to the emerging and rapidly increasing discipline of Gay and Lesbian studies. Ronald Long's reviewing and critiquing comments are "partisan," in the best sense of the word, to the point, and do not mince words.

In the part of this volume entitled *Families and Coalitions: Lesbians and Gay Men Creating New Patterns of Community* the collected essays tackle issues addressing relationships, concepts of family, and patterns of community. Carter Heyward, Mary Hunt, Elizabeth Say, Mark Kowalewski, and I, we all look at the critical issues from our particular perspectives which have been shaped by our respective experiences as Lesbian women or Gay men in a white male dominated, heterosexually defined, and patriarchically ruled world. In this world the concepts of relationship and community and the idea of family have been designed, legitimized, and institutionalized by those in possession of the power monopoly. Relationships of love–creating and justice–making are disregarded in such a world in favor of the institutionalization of hierarchical power, systemic exploitation of women and children, and oppression on non–canonic, i.e., "deviant" ethnic or sexual orientation minority populations.

This, however, does not mean that everything is in plain and simple harmony between Gay men and Lesbians. Particularly the essays of Carter Heyward and Mary Hunt point in unambiguous ways and, at times, in reprimanding tone to the differences and divergences that still exist even within the communities of Gay people, particularly the appalling sexism among many Gay men. But they also point to the tendency to unhealthy body and sexuality enmity of many a Lesbian/Feminist woman. The contributions of Mark Kowalewski, Elizabeth Say and myself are concerned with a fundamental critique of the traditional concept of family. They investigate the possibilities for the deconstruction of an oppressive concept with its attached social institution and the subsequent reconstruction of an idea of family which will be commensurate with the demands of Lesbians and Gay men for freedom and their longing for the establishment of a non–exploitative social reality.

At the 1992 AAR annual meeting in San Francisco we were convinced that times were about to change for the better for Gay/Lesbian/Bi–people in the United States and for all groups of people who are marginalized because of who they are. The dozen dark years of the Reagan–Bush debacle weighed heavily on our shoulders, yet we had not lost hope, we had not given up on our struggle and our lives. The Clinton–Gore presidential election victory was still very fresh in our minds and I hope I am correct in describing the collective mood at our program sessions as upbeat and replete with positive expectations of the newly elected Democratic administration.

A year after the electoral victory the flowers of victory have wilted, the champagne has lost its sparkle, and the rosy colors of the picture of our political expectations have faded almost beyond recognition. Our exuberance has given way to sobriety, our joy about impending change was muffled by the forces of political reality, expediency, and unethical compromise.

The ban on Gays in the armed forces has not been lifted, worse, it now has been written into law by a Congress whose members are more interested in placating the rampant homohatred, to use Mary Hunt's expression, of small, nevertheless noisy parts of their constituency. The issue of lifting the ban was thereby *de facto* taken out of the administrative hands of the President as the Commander–in–Chief and it will now be more difficult to challenge the constitutionality of the codified ban in the courts.

A number of of states are under pressure from right-wing religious groups to amend their constitutions with an anti-Gay clause *à la* Colorado Amendment 2. Similar measures have been introduced and, unfortunately, passed in a number of smaller county or municipal legislatures. These anti-Gay measures target specifically identified groups of citizens and deny them the right to appeal to the protection of the constitution whenever their civil rights, their lives, and their liberty are under attack.

It is into this dire situation that the present volume is released. The editors wish wholeheartedly that the essays contained in this book provide a significant contribution to the study and discussion of issues of great social and political, religious and spiritual concern to Gay people and to society at large.

Mt. Pleasant, Michigan
11 October 1993
National Coming Out Day

Part A

Gay Spirituality, AIDS,
and Ecclesiology

I. Susan E. Henking:

The Legacies of AIDS: Religion and Mourning in AIDS-Related Memoirs*

> *What we need are art forms that might symbolize our sacred Union, allowing us to identify with our struggle.*
>
> *Day after day, we must burn our Trojan horse to ashes and in its place construct the Ark of our Covenant. The war memorial to those felled by AIDS should logically resemble the Wailing Wall, where true believers pray in memory of ordeals visited upon their people by God. Like Job, we should refuse to curse our fate, instead devoting all of our strength to surviving until God and the devil tire of tormenting us and the virus is expelled from our desecrated Temple.[1]*

In the decade plus which has passed since the initial recognition of unusual cases of Kaposi's sarcoma and pneumocystis pneumonia among young, white, urban, homosexual men,[2] AIDS and HIV infection have become the topic of widespread and volatile debate. Among the many voices which have clamored for attention have been people living with AIDS, their carepartners[3] and loved ones, and their allies. While this diverse group has spoken in a wide range of contexts and with many voices, they have also spoken in a new sort of autobiographical act—the AIDS-related memoir. This broadly defined category includes a range of published and unpublished material by people living with AIDS, by scientists and hospice workers, by parents and lovers of the HIV-infected.[4]

As represented in such memoirs, people with AIDS and those around them negotiate their entry into the world of AIDS with particular attention to religion. Indeed, these texts remind us that, in the EuroAmerican context, AIDS and HIV infection are sites of ongoing cultural controversy regarding the construction of religion. More generally, AIDS-related memoirs represent the complex intertwining of loss with the construction of meanings—and subjectivities—in the age of AIDS.[5]

While individual memoirs often depend upon dominant cultural narratives and, hence, problematic claims based on the authority of experience, read together these materials offer us the possibility of a collective memory which is a countermemory. Read alongside one another, they resist the totalizing potential of isolated examples, offering repeated—yet radically dissimilar—representations of the "paradoxical individuality of the exemplum" and serving as a reminder that "we can employ 'experience' as a signifier to mark not private and interior knowledges but the intersection between such knowledges and the collective, public structures that frame them."[6] When read together, then, AIDS-related memoirs offer insight into the variety of ways EuroAmericans have negotiated religious identities in a secular world and sexual identities in an era of (potentially) lethal sex.

1. Representing Religion in AIDS-related Memoirs

According to medical sociologist Rose Weitz, a key problem for those who face the possibility—and reality—of a diagnosis with HIV infection or AIDS is uncertainty. Strategies to cope with that uncertainty and/or exercise control become crucial. While these strategies vary from person to person and from one stage of the illness to another, Weitz argues that persons with HIV disease cope with uncertainty by developing normative frameworks that make their situations comprehensible.[7] Weitz's interview data show that persons with AIDS—and those around them—draw upon a variety of culturally available resources in constructing such normative frameworks.

It is not surprising, then, that many AIDS-related memoirs attend to religion. Nor is it surprising that they do so in a wide variety of ways, for religious groups have themselves responded to the AIDS crisis in many fashions.[8] The struggle to develop a normative framework requires an effort to make (or grasp) meaning in the face of apparent meaningless loss. In addition to frequent use of the language of magic and miracle, many explicitly struggle with the problems of God and death and reflect on the positive or negative role of institutionalized religion in their lives. Others offer their stories as a witness to an alternative to conventional forms of religion—either a reformed version of their tradition or a less conventional "spiritual" approach. Many, indeed, describe the writing of memoirs as the creation of a legacy; this effort is, itself, depicted as a religio-spiritual quest, an exercise in survival and in the struggle for meaning.

a. From Punishment to Compassion:

As Weitz notes, "the search for meaning is often a painful one, set as it is in the context of popular belief that HIV disease is punishment for sin."[9] Like many of us, memoirists remember that Jerry Falwell said that "AIDS is a lethal judgment of God on the sin of homosexuality and it is also the judgment of God on America for endorsing this vulgar, perverted and reprobate lifestyle."[10] Indeed, many memoirists indicate that hostile rejection and fear of people with AIDS—and of homosexuality—is an ongoing reality of their everyday lives, often justified by religious perspectives. For many—both gay and nongay—this requires a struggle not to reject themselves.[11]

While memoirs by—and about—gay men are particularly likely to attend to linkages between religion and homophobic discrimination, nongay memoirists, including Ryan White, also testify to the negative impact of national religious commentators and to their rejection by local congregations on the grounds of arguments about divine punishment.[12] Many point to the roles of Roman Catholicism and Protestant fundamentalism in articulating—and enforcing—such an interpretation of AIDS. For some, this leads to vitriolic rejection of Christianity; indeed, some argue that the church has made religion impossible for gay men.[13] For others, the impact of religion is neither monolithically nor simply negative. Memoirists like Ryan White, for example, find religion, church, prayer and, on occasion, clergy helpful. For them, the theme of (religious) compassion stands over against reduction of religion to the motif of divine punishment.[14]

Jews and Christians who call for compassion argue that divine punishment models of the AIDS epidemic are neither justifiable biblically nor theologically. Often the struggle against the divine punishment model is formulated as a struggle to articulate a different model of God (or Christ). Like Barbara Peabody, mother of a person with AIDS and author of the AIDS-related memoir, *The Screaming Room*, those who articulate a call for compassion ask,

> if the essence of Christianity is unconditional love, how can these fervent disciples of Christ make their love conditional...[15]

Similarly, Dan Turner, the second man with Kaposi's sarcoma in San Francisco General Hospital, says:

> The AIDS epidemic is only an advantage for the Christian right if we cower and let

> it be. Our attitude should topple theirs by
> virtue of Christ's example of caring for
> the sick. He didn't go around Galilee
> trying to change people's sexual prefer-
> ence.[16]

Since formulations of the meaning of religious community often follow from understandings of God, the
effort at theodicy involves, for some, the attempt to
reform the church (or synagogue)—drawing on the
Metropolitan Community Church, Dignity, Integrity,
and Interfaith Networks, for example.[17] In a related
move, Shireen Perry's book, *In Sickness and in
Health,* depicts a supportive church community which
is crucial for Shireen and her (ex-gay) husband as
they struggle with AIDS. Her book concludes with
the following remark:

> Asked at the end of their last CBN inter-
> view what they thought AIDS patients and
> their loved ones wanted from the people
> around them, Shireen said, "I think we
> want people, especially people in the
> church, just to have Christ's love and
> compassion rather than condemnation and
> judgment."[18]

For some authors, the movement from a model of
divine punishment to a model of compassion becomes central to their self-representation and their
memoir. Jerry Arterburn's complex story of evangelical Christianity, homosexuality and AIDS, for example, devotes substantial attention to his worry that
God had "turned his face from him" because of his
sins and that his illness was a judgment.[19] His rejection of this possibility and his commitment to evangelical Christianity are the core of the narrative. These
are simultaneously possible for Arterburn because,
rather than arguing against rejections of ho-

mosexuality, his narrative assumes—and endorses—such rejection.

During a second bout with pneumocystis pneumonia, Arterburn writes, he asked the Holy Spirit to run his life and found a way to persevere:

> I was going to say no to my doubts about God and his love and I was going to say yes to His love and my faith. I refused to listen to those who would have me believe that I was experiencing a form of punishment from God. I refused to accept the concept that what had happened was the judgment of God. I knew God wasn't 'getting back at me' because I was a homosexual. My getting AIDS is not an act of cruelty on the part of God. The destruction of my physical body may be complete, but my soul is reserved for heaven.[20]

Out of this transformation emerged Arterburn's understanding of God as a God of love, of guilt and sin as the common human experience, and of struggle as a universal human necessity. Most generally, he argues, God *is not* interested in punishment and *is* interested in forgiveness. While the homosexual sins, so do all humans. Thus, Christians must respond to persons with AIDS with compassion and those engaged in a homosexual lifestyle, Arterburn argues, must "come out" of homosexuality to a life in Christ.[21]

This reading of Arterburn reminds us that divine retribution constructions of the AIDS crisis are not simply *responses to* AIDS coming from those who stand *outside*. Rather, such responses exist *within* the communities of persons living with AIDS and, indeed, *within* persons who are themselves living with HIV disease.[22] Read against solutions offered by others, Arterburn's rejection of homosexuality also serves to problematize the authority of experience, reminding us that not all who narrate the legacies of AIDS are alike.

b. Alternative Spiritualities:

Rejection of the divine punishment model of disease does not lead all memoirists, of course, to embrace an argument (or identity) favoring (Christian) compassion and rejecting homosexuality. Indeed, not all memoirists embrace an argument favoring religion per se. For some, rejection of conventional religion is wholehearted. And yet, these authors, too, search for explanations. In doing so, they sometimes respond to the dilemmas posed by traditional religions by offering an alternative normative framework which they label "spirituality."[23]

In AIDS-related memoirs, many distinguish religion and spirituality by linking the former with accepted (usually Christian) institutions and the latter with a more individualized or psychologized search for wholeness or meaning. Most link religion to the notion of transcendence and emphasize embodiment, connectedness and immanence in their view of spirituality. Memoirists often invoke, for example, connections between physicality and spirituality.

"Life at best is brief," says Dan Turner,

> and a life-threatening illness can only make it seem more precious. To integrate the body, mind, and spirit in a productive whole has always been my goal.[24]

Paul Reed describes a related sense of the spiritual in *The Q Journal: A Treatment Diary.* Reed depicts the spiritual dimension as "universal," as more than "the material and the emotional" and discusses his experience of taking compound Q as affecting his spirit—"the deepest tangle of awareness, being, hope, love, essence." Like other authors, he argues that one of the characteristics of the long term AIDS patient is a "spiritual sense" or feeling that something exists beyond the self.[25] Similarly, Betty Clare Moffatt, author of *When Someone You Love Has AIDS*, and mother of Mike, who died from AIDS, draws upon the work of Dr. Robert Brooks. For Brooks—and for Moffatt—the "spiritual dimension" is about "connectedness... to feel like a part of the cosmos, to experience being a part of the whole."[26]

In rejecting religion in favor of something of this sort, such authors draw upon a wide array of cultural and religious resources. They offer, for example, formulations which parallel—and in some cases explicitly draw upon—literatures within gay and feminist theology.[27] More often, however, they adopt a more or less "new age" approach or create a more "individualized" spiritual formulation.

For some, positive thinking will bring healing. Betty Clare Moffatt (and her son, Mike), for example, emphasize spiritual healing, including the well-known "Course in Miracles." In Moffatt's view, healing requires spiritual change. Shifting from being a victim of circumstances to being the creator of experience, she writes,

> literally involves a willingness to experience one's *self* as being powerful enough to be the cause of one's own experience.[28]

Others use visualization or acupuncture, and the release of feelings as strategies which they understand as *both* therapeutic *and* "spiritual." Still others draw upon new age beliefs in multiple lives or reincarnation in creating a normative framework.[29]

In contrast to memoirs which draw upon such new age material are others which explicitly reject such a strategy. Though Monette's treatment of fundamentalism is peripheral and his rejection of new age formulations is explicit,[30] the overall trajectory of *Borrowed Time*, for example, does emphasize religion, redefined as "spirituality." In particular, Monette's awareness of links between male homosexuality and ancient Greece served as a resource to be drawn upon to support his love for Roger, which "became the only untouched shade in the dawning fireball, what Tillich calls God, the ground of being."[31] And yet, this resource too was something to question in the face of AIDS:

> The closest I came to believing something higher after the loss of the old Episcopal thing—happened in Greece, and centered on the Greek ideal: scholar, philosopher, athlete, warrior, citizen...it gave me a context. But how is that context still valid, when it seems like it only fits the joy of intensely living as R and I have been doing over the last years, all the Greek parts in flower. What's *left* of that ideal? Just Greek tragedy, the horrors of fate? How to be a Hero—the thing the Greeks believed in most.[32]

As depicted in the *Borrowed Time*, an emphasis upon immanence arose in tandem with this questioning; Monette writes:

> [Y]ou come to see there's something nearly sacred—a word I can't get the God out of, I know—about being a wound dresser. To be that intimate with flesh and blood, so close to the body's ache to heal, you learn how little to take for granted, defying death in the bargain. You are an instrument, and your engine is concentration. There's not a lot of room

for ego when you're swabbing the open
wound of an eye.[33]

Read alongside those memoirs which struggle with
the problem of God or attend primarily to the role of
conventional religious institutions, these memoirs
reinforce our recognition of the variety of frameworks drawn upon by persons with AIDS and those
around them. More broadly, their diversity points to
cultural disagreement regarding religion, spirituality
and their relation as well as the difficulty of seeking
meaning in a pluralistic setting.

c. A More Subtle Religiosity:

In addition to writing directly about such issues as
the problem of God, divine punishment and religious
compassion, and the need to refigure religion as
"spirituality," AIDS-related memoirs expand the
range of culturally accessible theodicy by depicting
(and enacting) the making of life stories as a religio-
spiritual endeavor. They do so in at least two ways—
by offering exemplary life stories which model personal transformations and by representing the act of
writing itself as such a religio-spiritual endeavor.
　In offering life stories which model personal
transformations, AIDS-related memoirs draw upon
conversion stories and coming out stories, hagiogra-
phy, holocaust memoirs and the tales of those who
have struggled with other illnesses. Thus, they draw
upon existing cultural narratives, including the narrative of redemptive suffering, in constituting their tales
of AIDS and HIV infection.
　In many of these narratives, personal transformation is a requirement. For some, survival is possible because meaningless life became meaningful in
the face of AIDS. Thus, in his memoir *Mortal
Embrace*, Emmanuel Dreuilhe writes,

To survive, you must die and be reborn in
a new incarnation of your own making:
aggressive, resolute, austere, and disci-
plined. If our pre-war persona doesn't
die away we ourselves die.[34]

In the intertwining of these themes, the person with
AIDS models not just the person born again but the
saint, martyr, prophet, or, indeed, Christ. In representing the experience of AIDS in this way, narrators
of AIDS-related memoirs describe what James L.
Miller has called the "ascetic route to
immortality."[35]

Carepartners and persons with AIDS alike utilize
this normative framework to comprehend the experiences of AIDS and HIV. In an interview with Lu
Chaikin, for example, she describes herself as having
(at least temporarily) "deified" a person with AIDS,
Gary Walsh. "Our relationship," she says,

provided me with the experience closest to
unconditional love that I'll probably ever
have in my life... We just opened up and
opened up to each other. It was like we
touched souls, literally. I know it's a
hackneyed phrase... By being himself, he
brought out the soft side in people who
would ordinarily just not let that out. So,
he just *was* love, you know? And by being
who he was—and he moved into that
more and more—he was transformed and
he transformed other people.[36]

Likewise, for Barbara Peabody, her son comes to
look like Christ on his deathbed.[37] Others offer special messages of a peculiarly prophetic sort, depicting
themselves as authoritative speakers in the age of
AIDS.[38] As Emmanuel Dreuilhe writes in representing his own life with AIDS,

> Sometimes I feel like a prophet preaching
> a humanitarian messianism, eager to help
> those who suffer from the same malady to
> follow my example and free themselves
> from the double tyranny of AIDS and
> society. It wouldn't take much to make
> me think I'd received a mission from on
> high to awaken our downtrodden
> patriotism, rousing them like Joan of Arc
> from their unconscious pessimism... I do
> not have a martyr's vocation, unless we're
> talking about those who go down
> fighting.[39]

For many the transformation of life—through redemptive suffering or political activism, increased
compassion or the new age—provides a context for
identity, a meaningful legacy and a meaningful death.
While risky in their exaltation of suffering and in the
temptation to univocality hidden within individual
message, AIDS-related memoirs which draw upon
such cultural narratives mark the life of the person
with AIDS at the intersection of "private and interior
knowledges" with "collective, public structures."[40]

Alongside such representations of culturally significant personal transformation, memoirists offer the
act of writing as itself a religio-spiritual endeavor;
writing becomes, often simultaneously, a form of
magic and a legacy for the future.[41] Emmanuel
Dreuilhe's work, *Mortal Embrace: Living with AIDS*,
is unusual in its extensive reflections on the act of
creating the text (though not in its emphasis on
writing as the creation of a legacy). Early on in the
book, Dreuilhe pushes against the univocal identity
some memoirs risk:

> This diary is a singular experience, but I
> have tried to present, in the manner of
> David Hockney's photographic mon-
> tages, a complete series of images of the

> same sickroom: that mental room which now forms the confined universe of people with AIDS, a room we will leave only to die. Here and there a detail may be arbitrarily enlarged, out of proportion to the other elements of the picture, because our perception of our own condition is uneven and discontinuous.
>
> During the months when I was writing this diary of AIDS, I was several different people, and each one speaks in turn upon the pages that follow...[42]

Later, he argues that writing is a way to stand up and be counted in his lifetime, rather than waiting for his obituary, and states that his "unconscious hope is that this book, sprung from my brain like a cancerous growth, will become a monstrous appendage easily excised from my body." Here, writing is not a form of therapy but a magical exercise, he argues, a form of verbal exorcism.[43] The "ritual act of writing gives me," Dreuilhe writes, "like David's slingshot, an unexpected advantage over the seemingly omnipotent adversary.

> Even if I do wind up dying of AIDS, like all the others, I'm no longer afraid of it, because these pages have purified me, given meaning—at least for me—to these last years of care, grief, and mourning, a meaning that is intensely personal.[44]

2. We All Mourn: Meaning Construction and the Work of Mourning

What are we to make of these narrations? As presented here, these materials direct our attention to controversies regarding the place of religion in contemporary Euro/America under the sign of AIDS. While individual examples vary in their overt message, read together these texts represent religion as a cultural practice and as a sign with multiple referents, multiple contents, multiple failures and multiple utilities. As autobiographical enactments, these texts locate such cultural controversy at the intersection of collective and individual memory. As responses to AIDS, each is also an effort at theodicy rooted in the work of mourning. In these memoirs, meaning and loss are not opposed. Rather, these autobiographical acts exemplify their complex intertwining in the making of narratives and subjectivities.

As such, AIDS-related memoirs are located in a third (transitional) space which, according to Peter Homans, is meaning; neither inner nor outer, constructed from past, present *and* future, this space "flourishes at the margins" and "cannot exist at the center ... without being itself destroyed." Here, "the unbearable complexities of transience are softened and made tolerable as the text becomes meaningful."[45] As individuated selves are made through the workings of memory, so narratives—perhaps especially the rapidly expanding collection of AIDS-related memoirs—link loss and meaning, collective and individual, sociohistorical and psychological, inner and outer. This is the role of monuments, which work to separate us and to bring us together.

For Homans, modernization and secularization involve mourning a common culture and creating meaning (and monuments) from that loss. Change is simultaneously forward moving and nostalgic, individual and collective. Thus,

Monuments engage the immediate, conscious experience of an aggregate of egos by re-presenting and mediating to them the lost cultural experiences of the past: the experiences of individuals, groups, their ideas and ideals, which coalesce into what can be called a collective memory... Monuments obviously bear an important, complex relation to the personal experience of mourning. Mourning is the mental and individual counterpart of the material and social character of monuments. Both are responses to loss... Even more important, mourning renders with great intensity and force what is perhaps the most fundamental of all human paradoxes: it is a heightened individualizing and interiorizing experience which is also accompanied by a profound—if only transient—sense of unity between oneself and all mankind... When understood in the context of monuments, the ability to mourn foreshadows the advent of individuation because it is, in its simplest sense, the capacity to support oneself internally while recognizing in full conscious awareness both the collectivizing and individualizing realities within which one inevitably exists.[46]

Built from memory, despair and hope, AIDS-related memoirs offer a legacy which seeks to fill the loss, both individual and collective, which is AIDS. As such, they exemplify the omnipresence—and ambivalence—of mourning within modernity and serve as reminders that memorialization and monument building are key—to culture, to selves, and to the making of what lies between, viz., meaning. As we read these narratives, we remember that *we all mourn.*

3. *Every Mourning is Different: AIDS, Homophobia, and the Work of Mourning*

And yet, AIDS-related memoirs—and their reflections on religion—do much more than exemplify humanity's ongoing construction of meaning at the graveside (whether literal or figurative). AIDS-related memoirs provide a reminder of the specificity of mourning in the age of AIDS. Here, the creation of meaning occurs within the paradoxical circumstance of a world depicted as both secular and religious, as prudish and sex-crazed. Here, "memory and desire are poignantly intertwined."[47]

In these memoirs, very particular deaths are portrayed: narrators represent their movement into the worlds of AIDS and HIV disease, a process which occurs in a context shaped by religion and, more particularly, by the negative moral status of illness (and HIV disease in particular), by homophobia, by racism and by sexism. As Douglas Crimp has noted, in a homophobic world, mourning for persons with AIDS (especially gay men) is difficult. For all EuroAmericans with AIDS, including those who create AIDS-related memoirs, the entanglements of the closet intrude upon grief. The cultural illegitimacy of much of what has been lost in the era of AIDS as well as cultural linkages between gay men and death complicate the work of mourning.[48]

To paraphrase Crimp, the autobiographical acts which are AIDS-related memoirs, when read together, call us to mourning, militancy *and* cultural production. Why? The authors—like those many who have produced the Quilt—remind us that mourning—and memorialization—are not simply the domain of hegemonic culture. Nor are they simply conservative. Rather such efforts are key for those of us who resist stigma and who must construct identities in the contexts of pluralism and domination.

Homans argues that meaning is *made* in acts of *creative nostalgia*.[49] Yet, we might say, with bell hooks, that "since decolonization as a political process is always a struggle to define ourselves in and beyond the act of resistance to domination, we are always in the process of both remembering the past even as we create new ways to imagine and make the future."[50] Like hooks, we might draw on Stuart Hall's perspective and say that cultural identity—including the identity of the person with AIDS—

> [i]s a matter of 'becoming' as well as 'being.' It belongs to the future as much as to the past. It is not something which already exists, transcending place, time, history, and culture. Cultural identities come from somewhere, have histories. But, like everything which is historical, they undergo constant transformation. Far from being eternally fixed in some essentialized past, they are subject to the continuous 'play' of history, culture and power. Far from being grounded in a mere 'recovery' of the past, which is waiting to be found, and which, when found, will secure our sense of ourselves into eternity, identities are the names we give to the different ways we are positioned by, and position ourselves within, the narrative of the past.[51]

In a parallel fashion, AIDS-related memoirs remind us of the complex intertwining of past, present and future, inner and outer, identity and its absence, literal and figurative, religious and secular in the worlds of AIDS. By focusing upon religion and spirituality, they direct our attention to a frequently invisible axis of difference and identity within EuroAmerican culture. In depicting a variety of negotiations of religious identity in a secular world (and secularizing identities in a religious world), they point beyond an understanding of religion as the site of nostalgia in a secular world toward the possibility of *creative resistance.*

Just as "safer sex" expands (and contracts) the meaning of sex in the age of AIDS, so these memoirs reveal the simultaneous expansion and contraction of meaning in a world of potentially lethal religion. Made manifest in the Names Project and the Quilt as well, the stories of AIDS contained in the burgeoning anthology of AIDS-related memoirs simultaneously move beyond the statistical to the individual, remind us of the multitudes who are gone, and exemplify the complex intertwining of sameness and difference in the age of AIDS. In sum, the vast variety of EuroAmerican AIDS-related memoirs reminds us that though we each mourn *every mourning is different.*[52]

* I am indebted to my colleague David Craig and students in Bidisciplinary 240 for the inspiration to work on these materials. I am also grateful for the useful comments of panel members and respondents at the 1992 national AAR meetings as well as Professors Carol Anderson, John Barbour, Betty Bayer, Claudette Columbus, Maureen Flynn, and Lee Quinby.

1 Emmanuel Dreuilhe, *Mortal Embrace: Living With AIDS.* Trans. Linda Coverdale. (New York: Hill and Wang, 1988), pp. 126, 155.

2 Of course, not all early cases were in this category. This linkage is associated with early reports in *Morbidity and Mortality Weekly* and early nomenclature like GRID (gay related immune deficiency). On June 5, 1981, this CDC-based journal reported on unusual cases of pneumocystis pneumonia in Los Angeles; on July 4, 1981, the same journal reported on 20 New York cases and 6 California cases of Kaposi's sarcoma among young homosexual men.

3 In her AIDS-related memoir, Fran Peavey offers this term as an alternative to "caregiver" on the grounds that "the care goes both ways in most of these relationships" *(A Shallow Pool of Time: An HIV+ Woman Grapples with the AIDS Epidemic* [Philadelphia: New Society Publishers, 1990], p. 89).

4 For the notion of autobiographical act, see Belle Brodzki and Celeste Schenck, eds., *Life/Lines: Theorizing Women's Autobiography* (Ithaca: Cornell University Press, 1988). On the analogous notion of autobiographical practices, see Shari Benstock, ed., *The Private Self: Theory and Practice of Women's Autobiographical Writings* (Chapel Hill: University of North Carolina Press, 1988). Under the category of AIDS-related memoir, I include those written by persons with HIV disease and those around them; I include diaries and interviews as well as autobiographies and memoirs per se. Unless subsumed within such a context, I have *not* included works which explicitly position themselves as works of fiction or poetry. While current discourse limits usage of the acronym "AIDS" to identifiable later stages of HIV infection, much of the popular literature continues to use "AIDS" as an umbrella term. For this reason, as well as the awkwardness of any term like "HIV-disease-and-AIDS-related memoirs," I have, somewhat hesitantly, used the term "AIDS-related memoirs." For a recent discussion of the variety of such autobiographical works see Marilyn Chandler, "Voices From the Front; Autobiography and AIDS," *a/b—Autobiography Studies* 6.1

(Spring 1991): 56ff. In addition to those already cited, published examples include: Jerry Arterburn (with Steve Arterburn), *How Will I Tell My Mother? A True Story of One Man's Battle with Homosexuality and AIDS* (Nashville: Thomas Nelson Publishers, 1988); Elizabeth Cox, *Thanksgiving: An AIDS Journal* (New York: Harper and Row, 1990); Elizabeth Glaser and Laura Palmer, *In the Absence of Angels: A Hollywood Family's Courageous Struggle* (New York: G.P. Putnam's Sons, 1991); Rock Hudson and Sara Davidson, *Rock Hudson: His Story* (New York: William Morrow and Co., 1986); Elaine Landau, *We Have AIDS* (New York: Franklin Watts, 1990); Tolbert McCarroll, *Morning Glory Babies* (New York: Simon and Schuster, 1988); Paul Monette, *Borrowed Time* (San Diego: Harcourt, Brace and Jovanovich, 1988); J.W. Money, *To All the Girls I've Loved Before: An AIDS Diary* (Boston: Alyson Publications, 1987); Barbara Peabody, *The Screaming Room: A Mother's Journal of Her Son's Struggle with AIDS—A True Story of Love, Dedication and Courage* (New York: Avon, 1986); Shireen Perry, *In Sickness and In Health: A Story of Love in the Shadow of AIDS* (Downer's Grove, IL: Intervarsity Press, 1989); Paul Reed, *The Q Journal: A Treatment Diary* (Berkeley, CA: Celestial Arts, 1991); and Ryan White and Ann Marie Cunningham, *Ryan White: My Own Story* (New York: Dial Books, 1991).

[5] Kent L. Sandstrom, among others, has noted that diagnosis with HIV infection has both interpersonal and subjective consequences. See his "Confronting Deadly Disease: The Drama of Identity Construction Among Gay Men with AIDS," *Journal of Contemporary Ethnography* 19.3 (Oct. 1990): 275ff.

[6] The delightful phrase, "the paradoxical individuality of the exemplum" comes from Jeff Nunokawa, "'All the Sad Young Men': AIDS and the Work of Mourning," *Inside/Out: Lesbian Theories, Gay Theories*, Diana Fuss, ed. (New York: Routledge, 1991), p. 313. The subsequent quotation comes from Thomas Yingling, "AIDS in America: Postmodern Governance, Identity and Experience," *Inside/Out: Lesbian Theories, Gay Theories*, p. 303.

[7] Rose Weitz, *Life with AIDS* (New Brunswick: Rutgers University Press, 1991), p. 78. On uncertainty, see Weitz, pp. 77-78. On control, see also, Patrick Haney, "Providing Empowerment to the Person with AIDS," *Social Work* 33 (May/June 1988): 215-253. Loss, guilt and the fear of death are, of course, also problems. See, in this regard, Sandstrom, pp. 275ff. For discussions of the impact of such

issues on those who care for people with AIDS, see also Joan Dunkel and Shellie Hatfield, "Countertransference Issues in Working with Persons with AIDS," *Social Work* 31.2 (Mar-Apr 1986): 114-117; and Marcia L. Martin and Jill Henry-Feeney, "Clinical Services to Persons with AIDS: The Parallel Nature of the Client and Worker Processes," *Clinical Social Work Journal* 17.4 (Winter 1989): 337ff. For a more general discussion of the relation of uncertainty to the development of normative frame works, see Peter L. Berger, *The Sacred Canopy* (Garden City, NY: Doubleday, Anchor, 1967). As noted by Susan J. Palmer, Berger does point directly to sexuality as a crucial area of nomization. See her "AIDS as Metaphor," *Society* (Jan/Feb. 1989): 44-45.

8 See Mark R. Kowalewski, "Religious Constructions of the AIDS Crisis," *Sociological Analysis* 51(1): 91-96; and Albert R. Jonsen and Jeff Stryker, eds., *The Social Impact of AIDS in the United States* (Washington, DC: National Academy Press, 1993), pp. 117-157.

9 Weitz, p. 67.

10 Cited in Kowalewski, p. 93. Dennis Altman has noted that "Jerry Falwell, whose Moral Majority is one of the best-known components of the new right, had denied saying that 'AIDS is the wrath of God upon homosexuals,' although many reporters claim to have heard him" (*AIDS in the Mind of America*, [Garden City, NY: Anchor Press, Doubleday, 1986], p. 67). Others cite the American Council of Christian Churches which has declared that AIDS is God's punishment against homosexuals. See Weitz, p. 22. Of course, Protestant Christianity is not the only religious tradition with this sort of understanding of illness as punishment. Kowalewski also cites examples from leaders with American Judaism and Roman Catholicism. In this regard, see also, Jonsen and Stryker.

11 The struggle not to reject oneself is apparent in an interview about Gary Walsh in which a close friend indicates that "he said that the Catholic Church kind of snuck in there every now and again, and he did go through periods of 'It's because I'm gay and God's punishing me'" (Nungesser, p. 196). In *Borrowed Time*, Paul Monette provides an insightful depiction of the impact of such struggles. He writes: "Seven years into the calamity, too many gay men have lost the will to love. The enemies of our people—fundamentalists of every stripe, totalitarians left and right—have all been allowed the full range of their twitching bigotry. Though gay men have begun to understand it is something in themselves these upright men so fear, too many of us have internalized their self-hatred as shame. That the flesh and the spirit are one

in love is none of the business of celibate men of God, especially those who believe they rule the province of love. But the mission of the homophobe is more pernicious even than his morality. He wants every one of us to be all alone, never to find his beloved friend" (pp. 124-125).

12 On the negative role of national religious commentators, see, e.g., White, p. 95. On local rejection on the grounds of divine punishment arguments, see, e.g., White, pp. 77 and pp. 112-113; and Landau, pp. 108-109. For a hemophiliac child's examination of whether his experience of AIDS is a punishment from God, see Oyler, pp. 73-75. For gay people responding to national religious commentators like Falwell, see, e.g., Monette, p. 166; and Lon G. Nungesser, *Epidemic of Courage: Facing AIDS in America* (New York: St. Martin's Press, 1986), pp. 88-89 and p. 213ff. Monette also points to the impact of fundamentalist families of origin; he writes of those who return to such families to die that they face "the worst of all, being deported back to the flat earth of a rural fundamentalist family, who spit their hate with folded hands, transfigured by the justice of their bumper-sticker God" (p. 205).

13 On this impossibility, see Nungesser pp. 87-89.

14 On the salience of themes of punishment and compassion in religious responses to AIDS, see Kowalewski, passim. and Jonsen and Stryker, pp. 117-157.

15 Peabody, p. 110. For another parent's efforts to address the problem of God as raised by a child with AIDS, see Oyler, p. 146.

16 Nungesser, p. 125.

17 For representative arguments from outside the literature of AIDS-related memoirs, see, e.g., Paul R. Johnson, "AIDS: Responsibility and Remedy," pp. 7-18 and William P. Zion, "AIDS and Homosexuality: Some Jewish and Christian Responses,"in *AIDS in Religious Perspective*, ed. William Closson James (Kingston, Ontario: Queen's Theological College, 1987), pp. 19-42. On the topic of community, see, e.g., Nungesser, pp. 243-244. Monette depicts a discussion of the divine punishment model which draws upon John Boswell's *Christianity, Social Tolerance, and Homosexuality*, thereby hinting at the importance of historical research as a third way to reject the divine punishment model (pp. 266-267).

18 Perry, pp. 186-187. See also pp. 181-182.

19 Arterburn, pp. 112-114.

20 Ibid., p. 116.

21 Ibid., p. 162.

22 Based on interviews with persons with AIDS, Weitz argues that many individuals with HIV disease "reject their rejecters as prejudiced or ignorant." However, she also notes that "...in the same way that members of other oppressed groups sometimes feel they deserve their oppression, [some people with HIV disease] suggest that at a less conscious level they do feel they are to blame for their illnesses... Others maintain that they do not deserve HIV disease, but use language that suggests considerable ambivalence... Still others have no doubt that they deserve HIV disease because of their 'immorality' or their lack of forethought in engaging in high risk behaviors" (pp. 68-69). In depicting some of her respondents, Weitz notes that those who cannot reduce stigma by arguing that God is a god of love who created gay people, sometimes offer (Goffmanesque) "apologies." She writes: "Instead of offering excuses for their behavior, these men and women first accept responsibility for their drug use or, more commonly, homosexuality and affirm their belief in the social norms that label those activities immoral. Second, they claim that they have reformed and are no longer the person who engaged in these activities. On this basis, they ask their families, churches, and God to accept their apologies, forgive their sins, and believe that the new persons they have become are their real selves" (p. 133).

23 See, in this regard, Abraham Maslow, *Religions, Values and Peak Experiences* (New York: Viking Penguin, 1964).

24 Nungesser, pp. 99-100.

25 Reed, pp.105, 123, 157ff.

26 Betty Clare Moffatt, *When Someone You Love Has AIDS: A Book of Hope for Family and Friends* (New York: New American Library, 1986), pp. 42ff.

27 For an example which does so explicitly, see J. Michael Clark, *Diary of a Southern Queen: An HIV+ Vision Quest* (Dallas: Monument Press, 1990).

28 Moffatt, p. 41.

29 For a religious studies perspective on the new age, see, e.g., Catherine Albanese, *America: Religions and Religion* 2nd ed. (Belmont, CA: Wadsworth Publishing Co., 1992), chapter 11. For exemplary autobiographical material see Nungesser, e.g., on visualization (pp. 106-107); on acupuncture (p. 92); and on the use of new age material regarding multiple lives, channeling, reincarnation, and the role of positive thinking (pp. 49-51). For a critique of these types of approaches, see Yingling, pp. 291-310.

30 See Monette, p. 227.

31 Ibid., p. 65. For his initial report of the trip to Greece, see pp. 21-22. On the ongoing relevance of the experience at Delphi, see p. 49, where Monette describes himself as praying to a pagan god and links his "blessings" to the experience at Delphi. For another example of a memoir by a gay man which draws on ancient Greece as a resource, see Dreuilhe, p. 116. For a discussion of the wider relevance of Greece to same sex spirituality, see Christine Downing, *Myths and Mysteries of Same-Sex Love* (New York: Continuum, 1989).

32 Monette, p. 105.

33 Monette, p. 263.

34 Dreuilhe, pp. 92, 97-98.

35 James L. Miller, "Acquired Immanent Divinity Syndrome," in Christine Overall and William P. Zion, eds., *Perspectives on AIDS: Ethical and Social Issues* (Toronto: Oxford University Press, 1991), p. 61. On the prophetic and/or pastoral role of gay organizations, see Altman, p. 86. Others argue that "AIDS raised basic issues of pastoral ministry that are prophetic," Earl E. Shelp, Ronald H. Sutherland, and Peter W.A. Mansell, *AIDS: Personal Stories in Pastoral Perspective* (New York: Pilgrim Press, 1986), p. 9.

36 Nungesser, pp. 179, 187. For a discussion of the representation of Gary Walsh, see Miller, pp. 60-61.

37 Peabody, p. 275.

38 In these regards see, e.g., Arterburn and Perry.

39 Dreuilhe, pp. 147-148. For another use of the image of martyr, see Monette, p. 44.

40 Yingling, p. 303.

41 Perhaps the best representation of this point appears in Susan Sontag and Howard Hodgkin, *The Way We Live Now* (New York: Noonday Press/Farrar, Strauss and Giroux, 1991), pp. 14-15. See also Cox, pp. 225ff.

42 Dreuilhe, p. 5.

43 Ibid., pp. 93, 139.

44 Ibid., pp. 149-150.

45 Peter Homans, *The Ability to Mourn: Disillusionment and the Social Origins of Psychoanalysis* (Chicago: University of Chicago Press, 1989), pp. 111-112; 336.

46 Ibid., pp. 277, 278. See also pp. 335-336.

47 John M. Clum, "'The Time Before the War': AIDS, Memory and Desire," *American Literature* 62 (4 Dec. 1990): 648. In concluding his discussion of the literature of AIDS within the gay community, Clum writes: "In AIDS literature, one cry of anguish comes from the 'Stonewall

generation,' who once thought it had found paradise and lost it through AIDS; another from a sadder, younger generation experiencing pain and loss without saving memories, present love, or dreams of a future. The older generation affirms the saving possibility of love to make present and future bearable, a possibility younger gay men seem never to have believed. For both generations, the urge to remember and affirm remains as a culture dwindles. It is that almost obsessive focus on memory—memory of desire—that is a central characteristic of gay literature in the Age of AIDS" (p. 667).

[48] Douglas Crimp, "Mourning and Militancy," *October* 51 (Winter 1989): 3-18. For a poignant representation of the equation between homosexuality and death during the 1950s in the United States, see Gregory Kolovakos, "The World Cleaved in Two," *Parnassus* 15 (1, 1989): 331-339. See also Nunokawa; Yingling; and Ellis Hanson, "Undead," pp. 324-340 in *Inside/Out: Lesbian Theories/Gay Theories.*

[49] The term is Robert M. Crunden's. See his *Ministers of Reform: The Progressives' Achievement in American Civilization, 1889-1920* (New York: Basic Books, 1982).

[50] bell hooks, *Black Looks: Race and Representation* (Boston: South End Press, 1992), pp. 4-5.

[51] Cited in ibid., p. 5.

[52] On the inadequacy of a reading of AIDS as simply a "universal symbol of the random nature of death," see Emmanuel S. Nelson, "AIDS and the American Novel," *Journal of American Culture* 13.1 (Spring 1990): 47-53.

II. Richard P. Hardy:

Persons Living With AIDS: Prophets of an Authentic Spirituality

Some people are vehemently opposed to the juxtaposition of AIDS and spirituality. James Miller notes
the tendency to see Persons Living with AIDS
(PLWA) as "victims" and to regard them as
"saints."[1] He remarks: "Whether the martyrologists
of the AIDS crisis realize it or not, they are forcing
PWAs to march across a violently apocalyptic terrain,
dragging a holy mountain of eschatological
baggage."[2] Indeed, we all should heed this warning.
However, much of what he says presupposes someone other than the PLWA foisting their own projec-
tions upon them. In this paper, I propose to allow
PLWA to speak for themselves about how they see
the elements of what we might call "spirituality" as
part of their human experience.[3] There is no doubt
that what I say in this paper does not cover the whole
gamut of experiences of all PLWA. Furthermore, it
does not pretend to speak for all PLWA. Each person
with one's whole background, personality and culture
offers a unique experience and expression of that
very experience. Nonetheless, what some have experienced and expressed is valid. It is my contention
that, in the particular experience which these PLWA
have, the spirituality which they live actually con-
fronts institutions and individuals who may not even
belong to any religious organizations, with an
authentic spirituality and challenges those institutions,
religions and people to let go of their controlling
mechanisms and live the God of the Gospels as
PLWA often do.
    As one reads this paper, one must never lose
sight of the anguish, suffering, horror and pain which

PLWA live day after day as they struggle against the virus within. Barbara Peabody's journal detailing her son Peter's struggle with HIV and AIDS is a monument to that pain and the joy which occasionally comes along during the process.[4] Those of us whose partners, children or friends have lived and died with AIDS know it all only too well. Yet, some (and perhaps many) PLWA provide us with an experience of something more—a self-transcendence in which along with the pain and frustration and continuing discouragement, they know a meaning which moves them out of self to other. The elements found in this self-transcendence are elements of a spirituality, which indeed enables them to discover their authentic self within.

1. Spirituality—A Meaning

Over the centuries, the Christian tradition has developed a lived sense of what eventually came to be called spirituality. Even within the scriptural era, the writers were concerned with how the reality of Jesus Christ and His message was to be lived by the believer. The "spiritual" person was one who lived this life in the Spirit of God (1 Cor 2:14-15). There was a wholeness, a unity of life in which the person (body and soul) lived here and now in the Spirit.[5] This was spirituality. In the patristic era, although the theologians of the Church kept their theology and their spirituality joined, there developed a suspicion of the body which led to the view that it should be subdued since it was somehow not as good as the soul.[6] With this dualism creeping in, it was not long before spirituality (which was meant to be everyone's domain) came to be the almost exclusive domain of the religious professionals, that is, priests, monks and nuns who created and maintained a hierarchy which controlled the uninitiated—the laity. Yet, by the Middle Ages, there was a concern that it had become too exclusive. So attempts were made to enable the laity to have a spirituality which was more suited to their own lifestyles. The Beguines and Begards in northern Europe and the later "Beatas" of Spain were the consequences of this effort. However, while the hopes were praiseworthy, very often the structure that took shape turned out to be but a kind of mini-monasticism in disguise.[7]

While much good came from these efforts, they could not succeed because they failed to address the fundamental problem of the dualism, the split between body and soul that had taken root in Christian spirituality by this time. Spirituality had come to signify "the other world," "things of the spirit," "a relationship with a God to be appeased," "an asceticism to mortify the body and rid the soul of attachment to worldly things." More and more, the term spiritual or spirituality referred to something in opposition to body or matter.[8] While great classical writers in the area of spirituality such as St. Teresa of Avila and St. John of the Cross had an integrative concept of things, the dualism of matter and spirit held sway.[9] We should add that even these extraordinary mystics did not entirely escape the influence of this dualism, at least in terms of the way they expressed themselves.[10]

However, with the advent of the twentieth century renewal of theology, beginning with the so-called Modernists and the development of historical theology, this other-worldly division gradually began to give way. This paved the way for a re-discovery of an incarnational spirituality—one that took body and life seriously. Thus, they cleared the path for the Second Vatican Council which made enormous strides in affirming the goodness of creation. Matthew Fox and his work in the area of creation spirituality has had a tremendous influence in this regard.[11] Feminist theologians, too, moved into a more integrated spirituality,[12] while the liberation spirituality approach has accented the experiential dimension of all human beings.[13] All these persons and movements have enabled the Christian community to re-discover the cosmic wholeness of life and the interdependence of all things which Jesus Christ presented in the very beginning. Above all, spirituality has begun to take the incarnation seriously.

2. *Spirituality as Integration*

The Dominican theologian Matthew Fox, has written extensively about what he calls "creation spirituality."[14] He attempts to move away from the dualistic, body and soul split, perfection-oriented spirituality by proclaiming a spirituality which is creation centered. Simply put: "Spirituality is a life-filled path, a spirit-filled way of living."[15] This way of life centers upon the interdependence, the mutuality of God, creation, and persons. In this spirituality, Fox maintains God is found in the four paths: the *via positiva,* where everyone and everything contains a "word of God"; the *via negativa* in which suffering, darkness and trials play a role in the process of meeting God; the *via creativa* in which our experience of the divine enables us to co-create; and, finally, the *via transformativa* where we act to relieve the darkness and injustice in the world and, in the process, discover the divine ever more deeply.[16] Here is a spirituality which does, indeed, take life and human experience seriously.

The spirituality of which we speak, then, is not to be seen in terms of opposition to materiality. Quite the contrary: "Christian spirituality at its best is materialistic, incarnational, a spirituality of the whole person in communion."[17] It is that which reveres life and all life experience. It is that which gives life. It is life lived in a commitment to an absolute value and within the Christian tradition, it is one's whole life lived within the context of commitment to Jesus

Christ, in his Spirit.[18] Leonard Doohan, though speaking of holiness, is, in fact, describing spirituality when he says: "Holiness is seen to be specified by one's condition in life and the laity living in the midst of everyday world events, family, politics, finance, sexual growth, parenthood and work are called to holiness *precisely in these conditions.*"[19] So, everything that happens is not only important but forms a vital part of the journey of the human person and of the whole human community to a fulfillment, even in this life here and now. No human experience escapes being part of the spirituality of the believer. Indeed, one's culture, sexual orientation, work, community—all form essential components of one's spirituality.[20]

Until the twentieth century, sexuality was more often than not seen as a hindrance to one's spirituality. How could it be otherwise in a mind-set which saw the body as something which weighed down the soul which aspired to "angelic" (bodiless) bliss? Hence, the accent placed upon the state of perfection which meant celibacy, along with poverty and obedience. Rather begrudgingly, sexuality was admitted to the spiritual experience only if it meant being able to produce offspring—the justification for this rather "animal instinct."[21] However, in the twentieth century, we not only came to understand that spirituality involves all elements of creation, but research and study in the area of sexual ethics contributed to a more holistic and integrated view of things.[22] Such studies enabled people to once again integrate spirituality and sexuality in a healthy way. Foremost among these studies, in my opinion, is Professor André Guindon's book *The Sexual Creators: An Ethical Proposal for Concerned Christians.*[23]

Guindon develops a sexual ethics based upon a "wholistic view of sexual selfhood" rather than upon the traditional dualistic interpretation (p. 22). He sees sexuality as a wholesome gift from God who is benevolent and "from whom nothing despicable proceeds" (p. 24). He does not speak of Jesus as one who judges others because of this or that infringement of the Law, but rather as one who affirms each person and his or her story. Consequently,

> The sexually integrated Christian lives in a world in which God seeks people who are accountable for themselves and for each other, people who speak an historically truthful sexual language. Such is the God of the Covenant revealed in the faith experience of those who seek Her. (p. 36)

This God, then, is a God of love who creates people attracted sexually to each other and determines that, "it is very good" (p. 25). The ultimate norm for sexual practices, indeed for all human activity, is love and "...In the intimacy of Jesus of Nazareth, those who are in need rediscover their full truth and learn anew to love themselves and to love others as themselves 'for the love of God'" (pp. 32-33).

Fulfillment lies in being who one is in love and truth (p. 46). Being gay is also a call to growth in authentically becoming who one is (pp. 164-67). Non-gays learn aspects of what it means to be human from gay and lesbian persons. The "disquieting otherness," which gay persons are, challenges non-gays to listen to what can be learned about living humanly from the very being of gay persons. Guindon goes on to say, "Contrary to many other groups, the North American homosexual community represents a sense of shared values and a willingness to assert sexuality as part of the whole of life" (p. 182).

Furthermore, "[l]ived in faith by a Christian, the gay sexual praxis is a commitment in the service of the larger enterprise of liberating the human so that God's image can shine forth in it" (p. 183; also see, pp. 178-79 and p. 185). Gay persons are, indeed, prophets who challenge the static conceptions of human life, especially when presented in what is thought to be a Christian faith context. Gay persons make all aware that hatred, violence and guilt-ridden sexuality are not the authentic Christian way, for love fills all with the value God intended.

In these approaches to sexuality and to spirituality, we need to be attentive to human experience as lived within a faith commitment because this is where we learn the integrating reality of a truly Christian lifestyle. Contemporary spirituality, which focuses on the unity of body and spirit, accents the mutuality between God and the human community. Thus, spirituality is the process of *living* with God, with others and the world in a faith which says that all is good and everything needed in the process is found in the concrete historical situations of individual persons and the community.

This being the case, what is the faith experience of PLWA to which all are called to listen? Within their experience of integrating mutuality, PLWA provide the community with yet another way of knowing God and the world. It is this experience that the human community is challenged to hear, if it is to grow in its image of God. Let us look at God, prayer, creation, relationship with others and religions within the experience of PLWA and thus, discover their prophetic role in the area of Christian spirituality.

3. *God of Love*

In a conference in Ottawa recently, William Marra, a professor at Fordham University, New York, spoke of AIDS as God's just punishment for Gay people because of their "disgusting sins."[24] For Marra and others within the fundamentalist segments of various religions, their god is indeed a cruel one. Gay people and PLWA often grew up being told that this was the

kind of God they were "to serve, obey and fear."[25]
Fortunately, however, such a god is but a figment of
the fundamentalists' own imaginations.[26] PLWA
have usually been able to see through such a monstrous human construct. Dan Turner in his interview
with Lon G. Nungesser says:

> The Moral Majority can use this disease
> against us and say it is God's plan or
> retribution, but theirs is a god of
> vengeance and mine is a god of love....
> The AIDS epidemic is only an advantage
> for the Christian Right if we cower and let
> it be. Our attitude should topple theirs by
> virtue of Christ's example of caring for
> the sick. He didn't go around Galilee
> trying to change people's sexual
> persuasion.[27]

What is important is the God who loves in and
through people.

Those PLWA for whom faith is an intimate part
of life have consistently seen the God of love. Ron
Russell-Coons said:

> In my journey some of the old traditional
> confessions of faith—simple statements
> about God: God is love, God loves
> unconditionally, with God there are no
> differences—have strengthened me and
> enabled me to move on... The
> unconditional love of God can be
> experienced through the very ones who
> have formerly been named the marginal
> "other."[28]

As Liberation Theology in the Third World has
pointed out, it is indeed most often the poor, the
oppressed and the marginalized who have

experienced the true God of the Gospels.[29] In all nations and cultures today, gay men and lesbians are part of the oppressed who discover the God who loves them *because* they are gay, not despite their orientation.[30] Gay men, lesbians and PLWA break through the fear-mongering religions to the God of Jesus Christ because they have accepted themselves as gift from this very God who prizes them. Having been able authentically to name who they are, they can authentically name God.[31]

They name God: lover, friend.[32] By this very fact, they acknowledge a mutuality between God and the human person. This mutuality breaks down the dualism and hierarchical structures which have weighed heavily upon humanity for so long. No longer is there the emphasis upon a God-over-and-above-us to the detriment of the God-with-us. PLWA have seen the mutuality which Jesus himself established by his very life and they take to heart Jesus' words: "A person can have no greater love than to lay down one's life for one's friends. *You* are my *Friends*" (Jn 15:13-14). Jesus himself wishes to relate to all persons as friends in a relationship of equals sharing and giving life to each other. In that relationship there is a healthy interdependence. There is a giving and a receiving through which each individual comes to recognize that not only is she or he not alone, but that each individual is necessarily bound up with others and with the whole of creation in the enjoyment and pursuit of a fully human life.

All can experience this because of the God they meet in others who incarnate Love. It is only because of this human experience of God in others as Love that the oppressed can dare to risk trusting that God is, indeed, as Jesus has said. Then, by naming God as God is, PLWA proclaim God to be Compassion, Love and *Forgiveness*. By that very proclamation they become the prophets who interfere with the injustice of naming the Christian god the god of vengeance, hate and judgement.[33] In other words, as Philip Kayal says:

> All around us, in the lives of gays, PWAs, and the volunteers, there are new images of god and new faces of the sacred at work that AIDS has generated and that the gay community sustains.[34]

4. *Prayer—Communing*

Because they experience God in this sense of mutuality and interdependence and are able to name God "Friend," PLWA understand their relationality with all human beings and creation. Consequently, there is the realization that in the process of becoming fully human—a process in which all persons are intimately involved, they and everyone else must learn to listen to others, to God and to creation. One way of listening which leads to acting is prayer.

Through prayer we enter into a consciousness of God's presence with and to the human community.[35] It is a process whereby human beings see and are grateful for the interconnectedness of all of reality. Katherine Zappone says:

> Meditations, even the simplest forms, focus our attentiveness on the self, and beyond the self. They help us to know experientially what we hope for in vision and activity: all beings interconnect through the power of life. We must cooperate with this power in order to sustain and be sustained.[36]

When she speaks of "meditations," Zappone includes all the various ways of communing with God, the "power of life" in whom all persons and things are connected. It is not an individualized experience. Prayer is the conscious entering into communion with God in whom all live. It becomes yet another way of being connected with people and things. It provides a new seeing into the goodness of all the elements of life.

PLWA express their own experience of prayer in particular ways. For example, Bill said:

> But I want to live now. I figure God's got plans for me, and as long as I make myself available to His plans, not mine, He's gonna keep me until He's through with me.... Right now, all I do is make myself available and try to listen to Him. When they say, "improve our conscious contact with God," it's done through prayers and meditation. The prayer is where I talk to God. But I just can't talk to Him all the time; I need the meditation. I need to listen to His word for me.[37]

In Bill's statement all the elements of authentic prayer are present. It is an awareness of God and an entering into a dialogue with that God. It involves a process in which one must express the self and all that is connected with the self to this God but also listen. It is both in expressing one's self (hopes, needs, wonder, concerns) and in listening that the awareness of God's activity, presence and life are known. But even with Bill, perhaps the most important part is listening. The listening is the contemplative part of prayer—a receiving.[38] It is being open to and taking in all that makes up one's life. Indeed, it becomes a rediscovery of life, self, God, and creation.[39] The PLWA who enters into this dynamic of mutuality changes, grows, and becomes more the one she/he is becoming with God. This prayer produces an awareness of the present moment, the now—and all that is found within it. At a recent Memorial Service called "Celebration of Life" held in Ottawa, a woman who lives with AIDS sent a message from her hospital bed telling those present of her experience of living each moment fully since her diagnosis. And she prayed that all who heard her message learn to listen and live each moment now. I have often heard PLWA speak in utter wonder of a daffodil coming up in the spring or the glistening snow or the mystery of people.[40] They do so because their developing contemplative stance enables them to *live now*, and to see all that is at any given time.

This approach moves them to life now and, consequently, to gratitude. Mary, a native person living with AIDS says: "I pray the traditional native way with tobacco... I think there is something wonderful about waking up in the morning and praying gratefully for the fact that you're alive."[41] Life takes on new meaning when one lives in prayer—provided that prayer is immersed in life, not directed toward a totally other world. Prayer roots one in flesh and blood existence. Lewis speaks of an experience he had after meditating

> When I opened my eyes, I said, "Gee, I am just like Jesus. That's why He came, why God sent Him here. We're supposed to find out what it is to be a human being." It was extraordinary. It was like a light bulb had gone on in my head.[42]

Prayer does not move one off into some "spirit" world, but rather concentrates one in this life. However, it is this life found now to have unlimited horizons because it is life with God, the source of life.

In their sense and practice of prayer, PLWA become prophets calling Christians to enter more fully into a relationship with God. This means not only that individuals and the Christian community speak, but most of all, it means that they listen. To be authentic, prayer needs to be focused in this present life, and to draw people to the realization that God is here—Emmanuel, God-with-us. If people realize this they also perceive that all individuals and all things are so interconnected in God that life is seen anew—"rediscovered"—and that it is good. By underlining their experience of prayer in some form or other, PLWA destroy the dualisms so often found in the prayer of Christians and Christian religions. There is no god beyond, "up there," demanding appeasement from the disobedient slaves. There is only a God living and loving with human beings in a process of mutuality whereby both come to a deeper life together. They challenge Christians to see prayer as a way of envisioning the world and life. With this attitude in prayer, PLWA call people to a new Christian spirituality which brings about an authentic lifestyle in which all can *live* fully *now*.

5. For Others

Those who have suffered and dared to enter that dark and painful reality, are able to feel with others in their pain. (And it does take a good deal of courage to do so.)[43] Compassion builds within them[44] because, somehow, suffering brings people together and makes them realize their interdependence.[45] God, others and the world come together in such a way that humanity discovers the value of every living person and knows that each one grows through inter-relationship and through being grounded in the Life Source.[46] This unity offers the possibility for transformation into the fully human being that everyone yearns to be.[47] It is no coincidence that so many PLWA speak of reaching out to others and being concerned about others.[48]

My partner who died in 1991 of complications from AIDS in San Francisco moved out to others. As I went through his papers after his death, I found a letter from the Shanti Project acknowledging his offer to do shiatsu massage for PLWA, on a volunteer basis—just a few months before his death. During the last year of his life, I found him becoming more and more concerned about the happiness of others in their journey. That active concern brought him to grow more fully into the person he was—one for others.

Each person expresses that concern differently. Bob Cecchi said:

> My real belief is that God takes care of those who take care of others, and as long as I take care of others, my health will remain pretty stable... We used to make key tags and I used to work ten or twelve hours a day, six days a week, and at least once every six months, I thought, "If it was only people rather than key tags that I was putting this amount of effort into." And now I'm doing that.[49]

Bob realizes that God is involved in a very real, incarnate sense in his own being for others.

Being concerned about others renews an individual and gives him or her a sense of wholeness. Dan Turner expresses this thought in a memorable way:

> I am more sensitive to the concerns of others, not as selfish as in the past, more likely to put myself out for others. I might tell people that I will say a prayer for them if they feel troubled. Since other people with AIDS have put themselves out for me, I feel good about sharing my experience with recently diagnosed individuals.... With death from AIDS surrounding us, my friends, my community, my feelings of care and

concern are broader and more inclusive than just concern for myself. I really care what happens to everyone else, and I admire their individual courage.... I like noting that gay men are strong men—especially emotionally—they are very caring men, and are not afraid to hug and hold on to one another in crisis. I would doubt that the love would flow as easily between other groups of people. Perhaps we have already been an example to those who do not understand our sexual persuasion. At least they can see the love we have for each other as people.[50]

Here, as in other testimonies, there is a sense of newness and growth which is not totally discontinuous with what went before. The growth which takes place is an enhancement of the person who was always there. It is a movement within the very process one was engaged in all along. Plus, it is something which takes place by accepting, and indeed, embracing all that one is. This includes, for example, the fact that one is gay. It is precisely in this acceptance and gratitude that one is prophetic. When men living with AIDS are able to show that they are gay, strong, loving, and caring, they witness to the very core of Christian reality: love for others. Rev. Steve Pieters, a PLWA speaking to gay men with AIDS says:

Be open to help and open to love and kindness. And to love itself. Get outside of yourself and do something for others. Believe in the possibilities. Believe in yourself. Love yourself, be loving toward yourself, whatever that means for you.[51]

It must be noted that this love is not some kind of self-sacrificing love that kills the humanity of the one loving. It is an authentic concern and care for the other which produces something positive within the one who loves. Lance Gaines expresses it this way: "Life was quantity, but now it's quality. I mean, for the first time in my life, I want to do things for other people. It makes me feel better now, to do things for other people."[52] There is a giving which is also a receiving. In the process both the helper and the helped grow in a true mutuality where "we encounter the divine by reaching out to our neighbor."[53]

In this sense, PLWA are prophets of yet another element of authentic spirituality—a love which destroys the dualistic hierarchy which so much spirituality espoused for centuries. Compassion replaces pity. Mutuality replaces inequality.[54] Indeed, this is the love which Jesus Christ taught as the very core of his Gospel. It is a love which he found in the marginalized.[55] It is not farfetched then to say that it is a love which he finds today in gay men living with AIDS.

6. Challenge to Religions

Homophobia is institutionalized within the very religions which speak of love as the primary commandment. That is why gay men, lesbians and PLWA speak of their deep sense of rejection by the churches which they had loved so deeply early on in life. Yet, that very rejection provides the strength which enables them to move beyond the rejection and into wholeness. The wholeness they achieve challenges these churches to become what they were meant to be: incarnations of the total, mutual love of God for humanity.

In Craig O'Neill and Kathleen Ritter's book, *Coming Out Within*, they discuss story after story of gays and lesbians who were expelled or rejected in a variety of ways by their Christian churches. There is Eli thrown out of the Mormon church for being gay.[56] Sr. Ann who, though being a lesbian, felt she could not only live within the Catholic church but actually influence it to change its attitude toward lesbians, came to discover this was impossible.[57] Then, there are Ellen and Lorraine expelled from their Protestant congregation for being loving partners[58] and the story of Randy, a native person, who not only was crushed by the oppressive attitude of his church toward gay men, but suffered because he was told that his native ways were evil and sinful.[59] O'Neill and Ritter point out how many gay men and lesbians who have told them their stories have undergone a transformation which enables them to live with God despite the rejection and condemnation which they have experienced from the institutional Christian churches.[60]

This is also the story of many gay men living with AIDS. The story of Paul Henderson who had been a seminarian in a Protestant denomination but was rejected for ordination when he declared he was gay, is most moving because he continued to work for the most rejected members of our society. He showed a path beyond institutional rejection, as did his father and mother.[61] Michael J. Christensen, an evangelical pastor who is chaplain of PLWA in San Francisco, details several stories of rejection of PLWA by various churches, including his own.[62] When asked about organized religion and himself, Lance Gaines said: "I'm not welcome in my Catholic church anymore. I was politely asked not to return to the church by the monsignor."[63] In referring to a friend who had died of complications from AIDS, Lu Chaikin said: "...he said the Catholic church kind of snuck in there every now and again, and he did go through periods of 'It's because I'm gay and God's punishing me.' And his parents, of course were no help at all. His mother wanted him to go back to the holy church and all that stuff."[64] Some PLWA develop a deep anger at organized religions.[65]

However, many develop a deeper sense of life with God. Some grow within various institutional religions and others outside them, but nonetheless faithfilled.[66] One poignant example is "A.J." Roosevelt who said:

> All my life I've told people that I'm an *extremely* religious person... but one who doesn't believe in the *church*. I can't help feeling that much about the church has contributed to the problems that we face with AIDS—especially black churches. But I think Christ had incredible lessons to teach us about what's important: loving each other, loving ourselves, and being active about that.[67]

The very core of Jesus' life and teachings become the center of life for PLWA. There is a faith which gives priority to people, love and life rather than to dogmatic orthodoxy. By being people of Faith, PLWA often challenge institutional religions to rediscover the heart of what they are meant to be—communities of love, mutuality, and interdependence in Jesus Christ.

PLWA have been through much pain simply because they have AIDS. Many experience an added pain because they are gay and/or drug users, and/or women, and/or part of a visible minority. By being what they are and perhaps because of what they are, they have become strong, mature and loving persons. In many cases they refuse to accept the judgement of others who say they are evil. Instead, they dare to affirm not only their own goodness, but the loving goodness of God in their lives and the lives of all human beings. This is often a hard pill for the churches to swallow. I think Stephen Pattison says it very well:

In fact, the existence of those who dwell in the shadow of the chaos of death yet are manifestly alive, refusing to behave as passive victims to be treated as objects of compassion, is simply infuriating to the institutionalized Church. It challenges its sense of meaning, goodness, power and control. The "dying" should passively ebb away into a tranquil eternity, not dance on the lids of their tombs, reject the cheap compassion of the Church and start giving it lessons about life, love and community in the present. The vision of a person fully alive, especially if regarded as immoral and sinful by virtue of sexual orientation or behavior, walking around, accepting themselves and others, being angry and assertive, is a deeply threatening and inconvenient one. It is such a vision which some people living closely with AIDS present.[68]

PLWA are then prophets. Though rejected by the institutions,[69] they continue to challenge them. The Churches are challenged because PLWA dare to say in a variety of ways, "You are not God. Nor can you limit God's concern and love. You have created a dogmatic god who is merely your idol, not the God of Jesus." In other words, PLWA do not beg. They dare to command the churches to become communities of love and thereby authentically reveal the God of Jesus who lives with believers in the Spirit of mutuality and interdependence.

7. *Conclusion*

The horrible tragedy of this pandemic called AIDS is frightening, but it has brought forward courageous persons who teach us how to live: PLWA. They do it by entering into their life context as fully as they can and living it. Because the majority of PLWA in North America are gay men or IV drug users, Blacks or Hispanics, or women, they knew what oppression and suffering meant even before they contracted AIDS.[70] Somehow, they have burst through it all to challenge believers to rediscover the God of the Gospels. By their distinct being-in-the-world, they speak a God of infinite love who lives with them because they are who they are. They proclaim a God who loves them in that very being. Their practice of prayer moves them into an intense appreciation of creation and life *now* in all its dimensions. Their experience allows them to move out to others in a variety of ways so that others may be liberated from pain and brokenness. They realize the interdependence of all human beings and live in that interrelationship and mutuality. Finally, these prophets call upon religions to let go of their power and their need to control and become more truly the incarnations of the God who lives with humanity. Theirs, therefore, is an authentic spirituality in line with some of the insights of incarnational spirituality, liberation spirituality, feminist spirituality and the more wholistic sexual ethics of moralists such as André Guindon.

The question is: Will the "good" believers dare to see and allow the God of Jesus to speak in PLWA? Or will they reject the prophets as they have done so often in the past? Do we dare to interact in mutuality, respect and discovery?[71] Whatever the answer, PLWA will continue to find God and life and, in that very process continue to be a challenge to those who profess to be Christians, but fear to live in that Source of Life.

1 See James Miller, "Acquired Immanent Divinity Syndrome," in Christine Overall and William P. Zion, eds., *Perspectives on AIDS: Ethical and Social Issues* (Oxford: Oxford University Press, 1991), pp. 55-74.

2 James Miller, p. 72.

3 Theology must start with the experience of human beings for it is here that the divine reveals the sacredness of the source of life. As John J. McNeill, "The Gay Response to AIDS: Becoming A Resurrection People," in *The Way* 28.4 (October 1988): 333 says, "... if we wish to know the theological and spiritual meaning of AIDS for gay men, this question has an empirical side to it. We must inquire what the theological and spiritual significance of AIDS is for those who are suffering from it!"

4 See Barbara Peabody, *The Screaming Room: A Mother's Journal of Her Son's Struggle with AIDS—A True Story of Love, Dedication, and Courage.*(New York: Avon Books, 1987), 280 pp.

5 See Thomas Deidun, "Beyond Dualisms: Paul on Sex, Sarx and Soma," in *The Way* 28.3 (July 1988): 195-205.

6 J. Michael Clark, "Patriarchy, Dualism, and Homophobia: Marginalization as Spiritual Challenge," in Michael L. Stemmeler and J. Michael Clark, eds., *Homophobia and the Judaeo-Christian Tradition* [Gay Men's Issues in Religious Studies Series. Vol. 1, American Academy of Religion] (Dallas, TX: Monument Press, 1990), pp. 51-52. See also Gary L. Chamberlain, "Response and Responsibility in a Time of AIDS," in *Chicago Studies* 29.2 (August 1990): 186-87.

7 Gustavo Gutiérrez gives a fine summary of this "monasticism of the laity" in his book *We Drink from Our Own Wells: The Spiritual Journey of a People* [Translated by Matthew J. O'Connell] (Maryknoll, NY: Orbis Books, 1985), p. 13. Also see note 13 on p. 140. For an excellent study of the spiritual movements in the Middle Ages see Jean Leclerq, François Vandenbroucke and Louis Bouyer, *La Spiritualité du Moyen Age* (Paris: Aubier, 1961), especially pp. 414-47, 573-601. Also see Michael Cox, *Handbook of Christian Spirituality: A Guide to Figures and Teachings from the Biblical Era to the Twentieth Century* (San Francisco, CA: Harper & Row, 1985), pp. 80-130; Otto Grundler, "Devotio Moderna," in Jill Raitt, Bernard McGinn and John Meyendorff, eds., *Christian Spirituality: High Middle Ages and Reformation* [Volume 17 of World Spirituality: An

Encyclopedic History of the Religious Quest] (New York:
Crossroad, 1988), pp. 176-93.

[8] See Jean Leclerq, "'Spiritualitas,'" in *Studi
Medievali* 31.1 (1962): 286-89, where he points out that
"spiritualitas" began to be used from around the middle of the
twelfth century to denote something immaterial as opposed to
material and how by the thirteenth century most texts used the
term in this way. Also see Sandra M. Schneiders, "Theology
and Spirituality: Strangers, Rivals, or Partners?," in *Horizons*
13.2 (Fall 1986): 258; Walter Principe, "Toward Defining
Spirituality," in *Studies in Religion/Sciences religieuses* 12.2
(Spring 1983): 130-31.

[9] See Leonard Doohan, *The Lay-Centered Church:
Theology and Spirituality* (Minneapolis, MN: Winston Press,
1984), especially pp. 92-103; Matthew Fox, *On Becoming a
Musical Mystical Bear: Spirituality American Style* (New
York, NY: Paulist Press, 1972), especially pp. ix-xxxiv; and
Sandra Schneiders, "Spirituality in the Academy," in Bradley
C. Hanson, ed., *Modern Christian Spirituality: Methodological
and Historical Essays* (Atlanta, GA: Scholars Press, 1990), pp.
15-37.

[10] See my study "John of the Cross: Loving the
World in Christ," in *Spiritual Life* 37.3 (Fall 1991): 161-72
and my more detailed study "Embodied Love in St. John of
the Cross," in Steven Payne, *St. John of the Cross* [Carmelite
Studies, Vol. 6] (Washington, DC: ICS Publications, 1992),
pp. 141-61.

[11] His first work, *On Becoming,* pointed out the
dualistic tendencies in Christian spirituality over the centuries
and began to express a spirituality which took creation more
seriously. His approach tries to rediscover the roots of
Christian spirituality in a more positive fashion. He has since
written several other works which attempt to add detail to his
earlier insights. One of his more recent works is *Creation
Spirituality: Liberating Gifts for the Peoples of the Earth* (San
Francisco, CA: Harper-San Francisco, 1991). While many have
disagreed with his approach, he nonetheless must be credited
with helping us take the incarnation more seriously when we
speak of spirituality.

[12] Katherine Zappone, *The Hope for Wholeness: A
Spirituality for Feminists* (Mystic, CT: Twenty-Third
Publications, 1991), provides a very fine synthesis of various
feminist scholars and their contributions to an integrated
spirituality. While there are many other feminists who have
done work in the area, I would like to underline the
contribution of Carter Heyward, especially in her two books,

Our Passion for Justice: Images of Power, Sexuality and Liberation (New York, NY: The Pilgrim Press, 1988) and *Touching Our Strength: The Erotic as Power and the Love of God* (San Francisco, CA: Harper & Row, 1989). Also see Joann Wolski Conn, ed., *Women's Spirituality: Resources for Christian Development* (New York, NY: Paulist Press, 1986).

[13] Here I would simply refer to the classic work by Gustavo Gutiérrez, *A Theology of Liberation: History, Politics and Salvation* [Translated and edited by Caridad Inda and John Eagleson] (Maryknoll, NY: Orbis Books, 1973), and his later development of the spirituality of liberation in *We Drink from Our Own Wells*. This is not to infer that other liberation theologians in Latin America, Asia, Africa and North America are unimportant. Each of them has contributed immensely to an incarnational perspective which sees creation as important, indeed as the meeting place between God and humanity. However, the limits of this paper make it impossible for me to give wide-ranging references to liberation theology.

[14] I have already referred above to his first and most recent books. Other than the numerous articles he has written, we might note some of his other works: *The Coming of the Cosmic Christ: The Healing of Mother Earth and the Birth of a Global Renaissance* (San Francisco, CA: Harper & Row, 1988); *Original Blessing: A Primer in Creation Spirituality* (Santa Fe, NM: Bear & Co., 1983); *Western Spirituality: Historical Roots, Ecumenical Routes* (Notre Dame, IN: Fides/Claretian, 1979); *Whee, We, Wee All the Way Home...: A Guide to the New Sensual Spirituality* (Wilmington, NC: Consortium Books, 1976); *A Spirituality Named Compassion and the Healing of the Global Village: Humpty Dumpty and Us* (Minneapolis, MN: Winston Press, 1979).

[15] Matthew Fox, *Creation Spirituality*, p. 11.

[16] Matthew Fox, *Creation Spirituality*, pp. 18-23. See also, Matthew Fox, "Sin, Salvation, Christ in the Perspective of the Via Negativa: A Theology of the Cross," in Roger S. Gotlieb, ed., *A New Creation: America's Contemporary Spiritual Voices* (New York, NY: Crossroad, 1990), pp. 21-37.

[17] Kenneth Leech, "'The Carnality of Grace': Sexuality, Spirituality and Pastoral Ministry," in James Woodward, ed., *Embracing the Chaos: Theological Responses to AIDS* (London: SPCK, 1990), p. 62. On mutuality and relationship, see Carter Heyward, *Touching Our Strength*, pp. 12-15 and p. 23. Also see Katherine Zappone, pp. 67-85 and pp. 113-45.

[18] See Michael Collins Reilly, *Spirituality for Mission* (New York, NY: Maryknoll, 1978), p. 25. But, Sandra Schneiders, in "Spirituality in the Academy," p. 23, speaks of Christian spirituality in the following way: "If the ultimate concern in God revealed in Jesus Christ and experienced through the gift of the Holy Spirit within the life of the Church, one is dealing with Christian spirituality." However, I have a caveat concerning the phrase "within the life of the Church." She would seem to be indicating that the institutional religious expressions of Christianity are absolutely essential at all times. I would question this affirmation unless she uses "Church" to accent the social dimensions of spirituality, and takes "Church" in its wider sense of "People of God." It is interesting to note that in her article "Theology and Spirituality," p. 266, she speaks of community, not Church: "We might define Christian spirituality as that particular actualization of the capacity for self-transcendence that is constituted by the substantial gift of the Holy Spirit establishing a life-giving relationship with God in Christ within the believing community." I find this earlier approach more acceptable because it accents the communitarian or ecclesial dimension rather than the ecclesiastical.

[19] Leonard Doohan, p. 41. Emphasis added.

[20] See Philip Sheldrake, *Spirituality & History: Questions of Interpretation and Method* (New York, NY: Crossroad, 1992), pp. 50-51. Also see Joan H. Timmerman, *Sexuality and Spiritual Growth* (New York, NY: Crossroad, 1992), pp. 33-34.

[21] For centuries procreation was the only reason for sexual relations in the Judaeo-Christian tradition. By failing to affirm clearly the essential element of *human* loving in sexual relations, integration and truly human mutuality were made impossible. They saw it as a sin to separate sexual relations from procreation, but one can find little affirmation in their writings of the sinfulness of separating sexual relations from love.

[22] J. Michael Clark, in his book *A Defiant Celebration* (Garland, TX: Tangelwuld Press, 1990), gives an excellent synthesis of various studies which in fact reconstruct gay sexual integration. See pp. 28-34.

[23] André Guindon is a Professor of Ethics at Saint Paul University, Ottawa, Canada. His exceptional study *The Sexual Creators: An Ethical Proposal for Concerned Christians* (Lanham, MD: University Press of America, 1986) has led the Roman Catholic Congregation for the Doctrine of

the Faith in Rome to issue a warning against it. See *Origins* 21.36 (February 1992): 573-80. His detailed research provides a liberating view of Christian sexuality, which some Roman authorities evidently fear. Other scholars have done similar work: see James B. Nelson, *Embodiment: An Approach to Sexuality and Christian Theology* (Minneapolis, MN: Augsburg Publishing House, 1978) and his other work, *The Intimate Connection: Male Sexuality, Masculine Spirituality* (Philadelphia, PA: The Westminster Press, 1988). However, Guindon is the main scholar in the Roman Catholic tradition. [*Editors' note:* References to André Guindon's book *The Sexual Creators: An Ethical Proposal for Concerned Christians* are noted parenthetically in the immediately ensuing discussion.]

24 See Sherri Davis-Barron, "Professor Sees AIDS as Punishing Homosexuals," in *The Ottawa Citizen,* Sunday, May 3, 1992, p. A9.

25 Lewis, a PLWA says in Perry Tilleraas, *Circle of Hope: Our Stories of AIDS, Addiction, and Recovery* (San Francisco, CA: Harper & Row, 1990), p. 275: "I went to church because I had to go. It was a church of the Catholic God who was a punishing God, who blinded you, crippled you, and was very vengeful." Also see Mark Pryce, "New Showings: God Revealed in Friendship," in James Woodward, ed., *Embracing the Chaos,* pp. 49-50, for a fine description of the judging and punishing god which so many gay men and lesbians have had to struggle with because of righteous Christians. See as well Craig O'Neill and Kathleen Ritter, *Coming Out Within: Stages of Spiritual Awakening for Lesbians and Gay Men* (San Francisco, CA: Harper-Collins, 1992), p. 181.

26 Philip M. Kayal, in his article "'Morals,' Medicine, and the AIDS Epidemic," in *Journal of Religion and Health* 24.3 (Fall 1985): 224, notes how the "vengeful and spiteful God is a social invention inconsistent with the 'God of Love' found in the New Testament." His whole article is a marvelous piece of analysis showing how moral judgements affect medical care, especially in the case of PLWA.

27 Lon G. Nungesser, *Epidemic of Courage: Facing AIDS in America* (New York, NY: St. Martin's Press, 1986), p. 99 and p. 112. Philip Kayal, "Healing Homophobia: Volunteerism and 'Sacredness' in AIDS," in *Journal of Religion and Health* 31.2 (Summer 1992): 127, says it marvelously: "...the sadistic God of authority, law, and punishment is clearly being rejected here. 'He' is being

replaced by a living and more just face of the sacred, a god of equality, love and justice. It is not we who have to be reconciled to a 'legalistic God' and 'Judge,' but rather a loving god who seeks our humanity and responds to us in our suffering.... Our god stays fast, is supportive of our needs, and leads us to renewal and change. To be authentically sacred is to be actively involved in the world, to change it, and to remake it with mercy and love."

[28] Letty M. Russell, ed., *The Church with AIDS: Renewal in the Midst of Crisis* (Louisville, KY: Westminster/John Knox Press, 1990), pp. 40-41. Rev. Steve Pieters says in Michael Callen, *Surviving AIDS* (New York, NY: Harper Perennial, 1991), p. 84: "Mine is a God of love, not a God of death. And so I believe that God wants us to be healthy, I believe that God is greater than AIDS." Another PLWA said in Perry Tilleraas, pp. 354-55: "Today, I am in touch with a very loving, forgiving, and gentle God.... So I don't see God as that ominous force anymore. I see Him as a light and I see Him as love. I see a piece of Him in everybody I meet. I see Him within me and with the things that I'm able to do today, like care about other people. I believe with every fiber in my body that we're His children.... I can make a mistake, and that doesn't diminish God's love for me."

[29] Earl E. Shelp and Ronald H. Sunderland have a striking section on God and the poor in their book *AIDS and the Church* (Philadelphia, PA: Westminster Press, 1987), pp. 76-90.

[30] Speaking of Bryan, a PLWA, Earl E. Shelp, Ronald H. Sunderland and Peter W. A. Mansell, MD, *AIDS: Personal Stories in Pastoral Perspective* (New York, NY: The Pilgrim Press, 1986), p. 70, say: "He has no doubt that God loves him. AIDS is not God's punishment on him. As far as Bryan is concerned, he has AIDS because he was unlucky. God, in his mind, accepts him as he is — gay. Bryan is certain that God provides for his current needs. His faith in God and God's love for him, in Bryan's words, 'will allow me to die a peaceful and serene death, soon if no cure for AIDS is found, or at a more distant time if there is a cure'." Also see Letty Russell, p. 62, and Stephen Pattison, "To the Churches with Love from the Lighthouse," in James Woodward, ed., *Embracing the Chaos,* p. 19.

[31] Matthew Fox, *Creation Spirituality,* p. 85: "Eckhart says that 'all names which the soul gives God, it receives from the knowledge of itself.' If this is true, then we had better name ourselves truthfully, or even God will be distorted along with all the other relationships in our lives."

32 Many PLWA experience that God is indeed their friend who cares for them with Infinite Love. See the stories of "Jim" (pp. 28-33), "Gary" (pp. 38-46), and "Alan" (pp. 60-65) in Earl Shelp, Ronald Sunderland and Peter Mansell.

33 Matthew Fox, *Creation Spirituality*, p. 23.

34 Philip Kayal, "Healing Homophobia," p. 121.

35 John J. McNeill, *Taking a Chance on God: Liberating Theology for Gays, Lesbians, and their Lovers, Families, and Friends* (Boston, MA: Beacon Press, 1988), p. 53: He addresses gay men and lesbians: "We need a profound personal awareness of God's love for us, but that awareness can only be achieved through a daily personal encounter with God in prayer.... We too can let go of all our fears if we can place ourselves in the arms of a God who loves us. The practice of daily prayer will help us to seek our home where Jesus is waiting for us, in our own hearts."

36 Katherine Zappone, p. 42.

37 Perry Tilleraas, p. 169.

38 St. John of the Cross says that contemplation is to receive, in *The Living Flame of Love*, III, 36, in Kieran Kavanaugh and Otilio Rodriguez, translators, *The Collected Works of St. John of the Cross* (Washington, DC: ICS Publications, 1991), p. 688.

39 See Craig O'Neill and Kathleen Ritter, p. 142: "Life can be rediscovered by being open to and receiving the lessons of nature — but you may have to sit quietly and listen."

40 A friend who had lost his eyesight as a result of complications from AIDS would ask me to describe the scene outside his window. He and others focus on all the beauty that is there every day. In fact, they tend to notice and take in everything, as John, PLWA, says in Earl Shelp, Ronald Sunderland and Peter Mansell, p. 91. In so doing, they make those who are with them see things more consciously as well. See "Lloyd," in James Woodward, ed., *Embracing the Chaos*, p. 33.

41 Perry Tilleraas, p. 30.

42 Ibid., p. 290.

43 In reference to PLWA, Grace Jantzen says in "AIDS, Shame and Suffering," in James Woodward, ed., *Embracing the Chaos*, p. 28: "How can anyone not in their position begin to grasp the level of courage required to face their illness with dignity and without self-loathing?"

44 John J. McNeill, p. 101: "Compassion or empathy indicates a free, voluntary process of entering into the

sufferings of others in order to liberate them from their suffering."

45 Craig O'Neill and Kathleen Ritter, p. 210: "Accompanying acceptance of life as a process comes the realization of the interconnectedness of all beings."

46 See Katherine Zappone, p. 25.

47 Craig O'Neill and Kathleen Ritter underline this interrerlationship as a reaching out which transforms, p. 228: "In addition to needing support for yourself, your own journey toward healing requires that you listen to and assist others. Developing the ability to reach out and empathize is an essential ingredient for transformation."

48 See Earl Shelp, Ronald Sunderland and Peter Mansell, pp. 91-92.

49 Lon G. Nungesser, pp. 36-37, 49.

50 Ibid., pp. 95, 100.

51 Michael Callen, p. 89.

52 Lon G. Nungesser, p. 59. Helping others means for some PLWA becoming activists in education concerning AIDS or in other advocacy positions. See "Beverly," in James W. Dilley, Cheri Pies, Michael Helquist, eds., *Face to Face: A Guide to AIDS Counseling* (Berkeley, CA: AIDS Health Project, University of California, San Francisco, 1989), p. 354.

53 John J. McNeill, p. 97.

54 God loves Jesus as an equal and in the same way, Jesus loves all, thus establishing the equality (mutuality) of friends. See John 15:8-17 which is the very heart of the Christian reality.

55 See the story of the Good Samaritan (Luke 10:29-37); the rich man and Lazarus (Lk 16:19-31); the Pharisee and the publican (Lk 18:9-14); the Canaanite woman (Matthew 15:21-28). See as well the words of Jesus to his disciples about the world hating them (oppressed and marginalized) in Jn 15:18-20.

56 Craig O'Neill and Kathleen Ritter, pp. 69-71.

57 Ibid., pp. 65-66.

58 Ibid., pp. 112-14.

59 Ibid., pp. 181-84.

60 For similar ideas on loss and growth, see John Fortunato, *Embracing the Exile: Healing Journeys of Gay Christians* (New York, NY: Seabury Press, 1983) and J. Michael Clark, "Patriarchy, Dualism, and Homophobia," pp. 53-59.

61 See the article, "Love Story: How a Father and Son Discovered Each Other in the Shadow of AIDS," in *The Wall Street Journal,* Monday, March 16, 1992, p. 1. The article

details the relationship of Paul Henderson and his father Duncan during the last months of Paul's life. However, the earlier events with the church are also noted. The letters to the editor in response to the article reveal the deep love and also the oppressive homophobia which remain in our society.

[62] Michael J. Christensen, *The Samaritan's Imperative: Compassionate Ministry to People Living with AIDS* (Nashville, TN: Abingdon Press, 1991), p. 67 and p. 155, in particular.

[63] Lon G. Nungesser, p. 60.

[64] Ibid., p. 196.

[65] See "John," in Lon G. Nungesser, pp. 86-87.

[66] See Michael Callen, p. 160: "Ron," a Cherokee Indian, said: "I have found more spirituality through reading about Eastern philosophy and yoga and meditation and looking at my background. I'm a Cherokee Indian. I consider myself to be more of a New Age person who happens to believe in Christ — in a higher power." See also John Lorenzini, pp. 120-21; "Roberto," pp. 144-45; "Helmut," p. 150; "Eddie," p. 154; "David Schofield," p. 165-66; "Gary Mackler," pp. 177-78.

[67] Michael Callen, p. 111.

[68] Stephen Pattison, "To the Churches with Love from the Lighthouse," in James Woodward, ed., *Embracing the Chaos,* p. 15.

[69] I believe that it is accurate to say that PLWA are rejected by the institutional churches, despite all the fine statements of concern and sympathy for PLWA. See J. Gordon Melton, *The Churches Speak on AIDS: Official Statements from Religious Bodies and Ecumenical Organizations* (Detroit/New York/Fort Lauderdale/London: Gale Research Inc., 1989). Individuals and small organized groups in various Christian churches often are the antithesis of the "unofficial" position of rejection. The homophobia rampant in institutional churches lies at the root of this rejection. (See Philip M. Kayal, "Healing Homophobia," pp. 114-15.)

[70] It should also be noted that as AIDS moves into the Asian American community, they too come to endure yet another discrimination to add to that with which they are already familiar.

[71] See Carter Heyward, *Touching Our Strength,* p. 41.

III. Roger J. Corless:

Beyond Acceptance:
The Possibility of a Gay Male Spirituality
in the Mainstream Religions

1. The Problem and How to Solve it

> A distinguished rinpoche was giving teachings on one of the higher Tantras. After describing in detail how one visualized oneself in union with the consort, he cautioned that one had to be careful to retain one's sperm. About half of the students were women, and one of them asked how this applied to her, since, as she pointed out helpfully, she did not have any sperm. "Just reverse the symbolism" said the rinpoche.

A well-known nun sympathetic to gay issues, in an interview in the *U.S. Catholic*, stated that gay and lesbian catholics "...are a perfect example of people who are able to stay with a church or community that doesn't always appreciate them or what they do."[1]

The incident with the rinpoche indicates the strength of heterosexual, or phallogocentric,[2] presuppositions, within Tibetan Buddhism, which are so strong that attempts to question them may only be seen as questions *about* them. The rinpoche, otherwise learned and compassionate, was unable to deconstruct the tradition as he had received it. The quotation from the *U.S. Catholic* neatly states the position of openly gay and lesbian persons who remain in the Catholic Church. The most they can hope for, it seems, is acceptance.

A frequent response to either of these situations is the rejection of the tradition that supports them. Heterosexual women, and homosexual men and women, who find phallogocentrism and heterosexism so firmly entrenched in the mainstream religions, and wish to be more than merely tolerated, leave and go elsewhere—perhaps with sadness, not really wanting to discard the tradition as a whole, but seeing no other alternative.

In this essay I want to suggest such an alternative. I want to push the issue beyond acceptance and ask what positive contributions persons other than heterosexual males can bring to the mainstream religions, not in some ancillary capacity, but at the very heart of the traditions, re-framing them in such a way that the traditions can be refreshed, reformed and renewed.

What I will assay is an exercise in "theology."[3] In order to do this authentically, my presuppositions and methodology, while recognizably academic, will not be restricted to the pseudo-objectivity which has come to be regarded by academics as normative. I will speak not only from my scholarship but from my own experience, and this will on occasion involve the use of "I," "we," and "you" statements, rather than third-person constructions.[4] So as to stay within the range of subject matter which I know fairly well, I will focus on the Buddhist and Christian traditions, and in order to be reasonably sure that I am not projecting my personal experience as grand, universal abstractions, I will restrict my attention to gay males. If my exercise is judged to have any validity, I would then invite heterosexual women, lesbians, and persons skilled in traditions other than Buddhism and Christianity, to modify and expand my suggestions.

I will first try to uncover the pervasiveness of heterosexuality and phallogocentrism in Christian

and Buddhist spirituality, and, by examining its
structure or grammar, indicate that it is, on its own
terms, problematic, that is, both from a Buddhist and
a Christian point of view, doctrinally suspicious.
This project will take me most of the essay, but if it is
successful, it will have the important consequence of
demonstrating that we do not need to take seriously
the notion that gays must get themselves together and
act, or appear to act, like straights in order to fit in
with Buddhism and Christianity. It will shift the discourse away from the presumption that there is, from
the Buddhist and Christian perspectives, something
wrong with being gay, or, at best, something aberrant
that broad-minded heterosexuals can tolerate or
"accept," and ask what is deficient about the grammar
of traditional Buddhist and Christian spirituality, and
what gays can do to correct the deficiency.

In the final few paragraphs, I will briefly consider how the grammar of Buddhist and Christian
spirituality can be re-constituted using homosexual
(especially male homosexual) imagery.

2. Faking it in Church and Saṃgha

The Christian Church has a rich tradition of the use
of sexual symbolism in the mystical path, sometimes
regarding the end of the path as a spiritual marriage.[5]
It is generally given a scriptural basis in the presumed *sensus plenior* of *The Song of Songs,* in
which the bridegroom is understood as Christ and
the bride as the Christian, specifically as the soul of
the Christian. Since, in both Greek and Latin,
Christós/Christus is masculine and *psyché/anima is*
feminine, this symbolism is supported by the language most commonly used by Christian mystics.
This is a natural and appropriate symbolism for a de-
votional relationship when used by heterosexual
women, and it is on this basis that Saint Jerome so
vigorously recommends it to consecrated virgins:

Let the seclusion of your own chamber ever guard you; ever let the Bridegroom sport with you within. If you pray, you are speaking to your Spouse; if you read, He is speaking to you. When sleep falls on you, He will come behind the wall and will put His hand through the hole in the door and will touch your flesh. And you will awake and rise up and cry: "I am sick with love" (Song of Sol., 5:8).[6]

One of the most graphic illustrations of the structure is given by St. Teresa of Jesus:

I saw close to me toward my left side an angel in bodily form.... [T]he angel was...very beautiful, and his face was so aflame that he seemed to be one of those very sublime angels that appear to be all afire.... I saw in his hands a large golden dart and at the end of the iron tip there appeared to be a little fire. It seemed to me this angel plunged the dart several times into my heart and that it reached deep within me.... The pain was so great that it made me moan, and the sweetness this greatest pain caused me was so superabundant that there is no desire capable of taking it away.... The loving exchange that takes place between the soul and God is so sweet that I beg Him in His goodness to give a taste of this love to anyone who thinks I am lying. On the day when this lasted I went about as though stupefied.[7]

The symbolism is that of a heterosexually induced female orgasm, as was so clearly understood by

Bernini in his famous statue of "Teresa in Ecstasy" which is housed in the church of S. Maria del Vittore in Rome.[8] A male who wishes to adopt this symbolism must, somehow, ignore his biological sex and imagine himself as a woman. Saint John of the Cross, who was Saint Teresa's contemporary, has left us a remarkable piece of symbolic legerdemain in his *Spiritual Canticle*, a detailed exposition of what he regarded as the bridal mysticism of *The Song of Songs*, in which he is able to retain his sexual identity by, time and time again, and always at the very last moment, shifting into third-person language. Whereas Teresa can say "the angel plunged the dart into me", John comments "In this stanza, the bride says..."[9]

Sexual symbolism in Buddhist mysticism is confined to the Vajrayāna, and is more common and explicit in Inner Asian (Tibeto-Mongolian) *rgyud* (Tantra) than East Asian Chen-yen or Shingon. The symbolism is the opposite of the Christian: the practitioner is, or imagines herself to be, male, and the referent of union is female. The theoretical basis is the statement that pure or enlightened mind has two aspects: great wisdom (*mahāprajñā*) and great compassion (*mahākaruṇā*). These two aspects are mentioned in all lineages of Buddhism, but they are given a particular structural weight in Inner Asian Buddhism. The two great explanatory systems of Mahāyāna, Mādhyamika and Yogācāra, are assigned to, respectively, Mañjuśrī, the bodhisattva of wisdom, and Maitreya, one of the bodhisattvas of compassion. These bodhisattvas are understood to have transmitted the systems to the human teachers Nāgārjuna and Asaṅga who, in the iconic representations of the Gelugpa lineage or refuge tree, are placed on either side of the root guru Tsongkhapa, above the Dharma Protectors and Hīnayāna teachers, and below the Vajrayāna teachers. Wisdom is then regarded as passive and female, and compassion is viewed as active and male, and is further identified with skillful means (*upāya-kauśalya*) or appropriate lysiological (*lúsis*, liberation) method (Chinese: *fang-pien*). The polarity which is thus established in regard to doctrine at the Mahāyāna level is worked out liturgically at the Vajrayāna level in the *yab-yum* (father-mother) visualizations of heterosexual union and the manipulation of the thunderbolt (*vajra*, symbolizing method) and bell (*ghaṇṭā*, symbolizing wisdom), which are held in the right and left hands respectively during the recitation of certain mantras.[10]

The symbolism seems to be that wisdom (the female, the openness of *śūnyatā* [emptiness], the womb, the hollow bell waiting to be struck or entered) knows *what* to do for the liberation of beings, but does not know *how* to do it, or does not have the energy to do it—it needs penetrating, activating or fertilizing by the male thunderbolt. Thus, despite the enantiomorphism between Buddhist *yab-yum* symbolism and Christian bridal symbolism, real power resides, in both cases, in the male.[11]

What, then, is the grammar of this symbolism? That is, who does what, and with what, and to whom?[12]

On the theoretical level, there is a threefold *différance* between the practitioner (or worshipper) and the goal. First, there is an opposition between the familiar and the mysterious: not only is the Buddhist not a Buddha and the Christian not God, but the Buddhas and God are as distant and other as "the enigmatic female" is from the standard-issue heterosexual male. Secondly, the male side of the relationship is active, while the female side is passive. Thirdly, the male side dominates, controls, and gives his power, while the female side is submissive and is required, if she has any power, to give it up.

The power gradient of control is a translation into the mystical realm of the political and social reality in which the woman has a legal obligation to be faithful to the man, as his possession, and to continue his line by bearing what are known as "his" children.

This *différance* is eventually collapsed, but only when the symbolism is transcended: the Buddhist realizes the non-duality of saṃsāra and nirvāṇa, and the Christian, although not becoming God, acts, in the state of the spiritual marriage, with a will that is the same as God's will. While the symbolism is in place, however, it is dualist. This makes it problematic in both Buddhism and Christianity, for it appears to support a real distinction between saṃsāra and nirvāṇa,[13] making enlightenment impossible, and between divine and human nature, making the incarnation, in its Nicene understanding, impossible, and the deification or sanctification of the Christian unintelligible.

Then, on the experiential and practical level, there is the problem that, if we are gay males, heterosexual symbolism is ineffective. It is designed to work with erotic power, but it does not turn us on. As text, it is meaningless, as abstract as a discussion of the sex life of butterflies.

It might be supposed that the problems of this dichotomy disappear when the focus is shifted up and away, as it were, to include both parties in the single symbolic body of the androgyne. This is the move of the neo-Jungian, and it is not without its attractiveness.[14] However, the androgyne symbol merely internalizes, without deconstructing, the power gradient, making it less visible, and it continues to model the relationship in heterosexual and phallogocentric terms.

A homosexual alternative presents itself in the practice of "looking at youths" in Ṣūfism, which was ambiguously accepted by the Persians, but generally condemned by the Arabs.[15] Consider the following *ghazal* to a male cupbearer (*sāqī*):

The curling locks above your ear, my lad,
has [*sic*] set the world about *its* ears, my lad.
Who in the world is there could gaze on you

while heart and head remain unmoved, my
lad?
You are a moon who bears a cup, O slave;
you are a cypress in a gown, my lad.
A cypress next my art, a moon embraced,
I hold when you are in my arms, my lad.
Why do you strive so to be cruel, O slave?
Strive rather towards fidelity, my lad.
Tonight you've caught me in a snare, my
love,
since from my arms you flew last night, my
lad.
Oh, may you from your rubies grant a kiss
so sweet, and ever drink sweet wine, my lad.
Cease this oppression; seek not to do ill;
the Lord of Justice's near; be still, my lad.[16]

This is intended as a symbolic expression of the
poet's love for God.[17] It has the advantage of being
erotically accessible to a gay male, but the disadvan-
tage of retaining the power gradient. The cupbearer is
in an inferior position by means of his age, being
"the youthful ephebe, the 'sweet boy' (*shīrīn
pisar*)".[18] Sometimes, the object of love is a mature
warrior, but he is still a slave.[19] The social and political structure is that of a bearded, and therefore definitely masculine, man, who seeks to impose himself
upon a beardless, and therefore quasi-feminine, boy.

This power gradient, and the identification of
boys, slaves and women, all of whom were expected
to be the passive recipients of intercourse and were
presumed to derive no pleasure from it, was axiomatic in ancient Rome. While penetration of male
and female slaves, and boys, was acceptable practice,
it was considered horrifyingly unnatural for a freeborn adult male to be the recipient of anal intercourse
or, still worse, to engage in fellatio or cunnilingus.[20]
In seventeenth-century Japan, a similar "hierarchy
was central to all forms of Japanese male love and

presumed a male/superior, female/inferior hierarchy of sexual activity in which the female or boy (inferior) is penetrated by the adult male (superior)."[21] The only significant difference between Persia and Rome on the one hand, and Japan on the other, was the tonsorial symbol of when manhood had arrived, signalling that it was permissible for one to seduce boys but not to be oneself seduced. In Rome and Persia, it was the natural growth of the beard; in Japan, the shaving of the forelocks.[22]

It seems, then, that if we wish to have models of spirituality other than the heterosexual and phallogo-centric, we will have to invent them.

3. *Making it with Pan*

The most productive area in which to look for these new models is a variety of neo-paganism whose members call themselves fairies (sometimes spelled *faeries*[23]) or radical fairies.[24] Fairies are gay males who wish to celebrate the spirituality of sexuality in general and gay male sexuality in particular. They meet periodically in "gatherings" which are remarkable for their feelings of comradeship without the cruisiness which is frequently so evident between gay males in other social contexts.[25] Fairies are often characterized by a vigorous rejection of traditional religions, especially Buddhism and Christianity, and a self-conscious adoption of pagan-ish or druid-like rituals, customs and names, these last called "fairy names." But, none of this is taken seriously, indeed self-parody, the outrageous form of drag known as "genderfuck,"[26] and a general feeling that one has wandered into a spiritual variant of the Society for Creative Anachronism, are all part of the fun.[27] And, indeed, fun seems to be the name of the game, and it is contrasted with tales of the grim, party-pooper spirit of mainstream religion. The mode is what I call *pre-Axial.*

Karl Jaspers seems to have been the first to notice that there is a clustering of "founders of great world religions" around the sixth century B.C.E. He called the period the Axial Age, and tried to describe the change which he saw occurring at that time. In my interpretation of Jaspers, I claim that pre-Axial traditions are local (tribal), pro-cosmic, and celebratory, whereas Axial traditions, such as Buddhism and Christianity, are global (in theory, at least), acosmic, and lysiological.[28]

For the purposes of this essay, the significant distinction is that between celebration and lysiology. This is nicely caught by the gay poet James Broughton's statement, "Buddha was very down on desire. Broughton is very up on desire."[29] The pre-Axial view of desire is that it leads to pleasure, and so it cultivates and celebrates it. The Axial view is that desire leads to suffering (*duhkha*), and so it tries to subdue it or escape from it.[30] Axial traditions regard pre-Axial traditions as superficial. Pre-Axial traditions regard Axial traditions as pessimistic.

It is not my intent here to criticize either the pre-Axial or Axial traditions, or to favor one over the other, but to notice that, if you find yourself convinced by the Axial view that samsāra is suffering or that the created world is sinful, you may have a good time at a fairy gathering, but you will be unable to import its values directly into Buddhism or Christianity, for the fairy perspective does not take the First Noble Truth, or the Cross, seriously. Therefore, once again, you will be convinced that you need to invent an appropriate spirituality.

4. Re-making Church and Samgha

A mysticism or spirituality which uses images of heterosexual union is trying to say something about relationship. John Welwood has suggested that there has recently been a change in the way humans can view their relationships with each other.[31] His insight is so important that it deserves to be quoted *in extenso*:

> In previous eras, family and society dictated the form and function of the man/woman relationship. Parents chose a child's marriage partner on the basis of family interests rather than the child's personal wishes. Since marriage was designed mainly to serve family and society, the quality of the personal relationship between husband and wife was of secondary importance. If a marriage was unhappy, community pressure would hold it together.
>
> Only in the last few generations has this situation changed. Now that couples are increasingly removed from family, community, and widely shared values, there are few convincing *extrinsic* reasons for a man and a woman to sustain a life's journey together. Only the *intrinsic quality of their personal connection* can keep them going.[32] Now, for the first time in history, every couple is on their own—to discover how to build a healthy relationship, and to forge their own vision of how and why to be together. *It is important to appreciate just how new this situation is. We are all pioneers in this unexplored territory.*[33]

Welwood recognizes that what he has to say may pertain to homosexual relationships, but says "I have chosen to limit my focus to the male-female connection because it is the area of greatest personal interest and concern to me."[34] For a similar reason, I choose to focus on the male-male connection, and I wish to suggest that Welwood's remarks are even more germane to homosexual relationships than to heterosexual.

G. Rattray Taylor has argued that a society arranges its sexual laws primarily in terms of property and inheritance.[35] If the society is patrilineal, so that it is important to know who the father is, sexual activity (both heterosexual and homosexual, Taylor says) must be carefully controlled. The women must be kept under lock and key, so that we can be reasonably sure who is doing whom. Conversely, a matrilineal society can allow more sexual freedom, since we can all see who the mother is.

Taylor charts the swings, as he sees them, between what he calls "matrist" and "patrist" periods in the history of western culture.[36] He invents these words (somewhat apologetically) in order to indicate a society's bias towards identifying with either the mother or the father. In the larger picture, however, we surely must agree with the feminist scholars who regard western civilization as a whole, and therefore Christianity, as patriarchal and patrilineal. And Buddhism, it seems, is no different.

Taylor's suggestion allows us to explain the heterosexual assumptions of traditional Buddhist and Christian spirituality according to a Marxist perspective, noting that it is only recently that servile labor has ceased to be *necessarily* performed by slaves (who are supposed to have been abolished anyway), wives, or children, but, for preference, is carried out by machines or freeborn humans who are (ideally) paid a living wage. We can claim that the means of production allow us, now for the first time (as Welwood says), to see other humans as equals rather than as sources of energy.[37]

If all this is true, then gays and lesbians find themselves today in a uniquely prophetic situation. Homosexual activity has, by its very nature, nothing whatsoever to do with reproduction, so there is no need to contain homosexual activity within laws designed to insure the property of progeny. Further, if I don't need a wife and children to do my housework and run my farm, I don't need to make arrangements with subordinate humans to ensure a labor force. I can, therefore, as Welwood puts it, concentrate on the intrinsic quality of my personal connections with other humans.

Gays and lesbians today can, then, enter into relationships on the basis of true equality and mutuality, and offer our experience to the heterosexual community. Of course, we don't yet know how to do this. As Welwood says in the passage quoted above, "It is important to appreciate just how new this situation is."

So far in this essay I have tried to show that traditional systems have little or nothing to say about relationships which are by nature non-reproductive and non-hierarchical, and that, therefore, they are not only mute in regard to a spirituality that is appropriate for gays and lesbians, but, also, doctrinally problematic.

However, I don't want to leave the matter there, on a negative note. I want to propose the possibility, at this historical juncture, of developing a gay spirituality within the mainstream religions. The actual construction of such a spirituality is outside the scope of this essay. But, it might look something like this...

Let us go back to the fairies. Since Buddhism insists that birth, ageing, sickness and death are really (although not ultimately) suffering, and Christianity insists that sin is a real (although not final) separation from God, neither can accept unconditionally the validity of the let-it-all-hang-out pre-Axial monism of the fairies. Buddhism says: "Look closely, it is suffering, not joy." Christianity asks: "What is your god, is it the God who created you?" Yet, if a Buddhist regards nirvāṇa as a realm apart from saṃsāra, or if a Christian despises creation as if God had not made it and seen that it was good, they are being false to their traditions. The fairies may offer us a corrective to the heterosexual, phallogocentric dualism to which Axial acosmism is subject. Neither Buddhism nor Christianity is officially dualist, yet both often act as if they were. I have argued that, in Christianity, this occurs when theology is divorced from experience, and that balance is restored by the persons we call mystics.[38]

The Christian message is that there is everything, and then there is God. As William Temple, a former Archbishop of Canterbury, put it,

$$(God) - (The\ World) = God$$
but
$$(The\ World) - (God) = 0$$

This is lousy mathematics,[39] but it makes the point. Christianity goes beyond what it considers to be the preliminary insights of the pre-Axial systems, that there is divinity *in* the world, asks from where this divinity comes, and answers, "from elsewhere." Genesis chapters 1 and 2, each in their own way, posit a chaotic or unformed something which was dead until breathed on, or into, by God. The separation between God and the world is emphasized by theology and the connection between them, while admitted, is de-emphasized, apparently to avoid what would be regarded as a regression into pantheism (or pre-Axial, pro-cosmic monism). The mystics, however, report their experience of the connection, that—

> The world is charged with the grandeur
> of God.
> It will flame out, like shining from
> shook foil:[40]

—and, in the process, begin to sound pantheist, giving the theologians conniption fits. As *Christian* mystics, however, they are not pantheists, they have faced up to the Axial truth of the Cross, and have gone through it to the resurrection. They have been buried with Christ and risen with him, bearing Gaia transfigured.

A similar case could be made, I think, for Buddhism. Although the split between saṃsāra and nirvāṇa is not as firmly drawn as that between God and the world, such that Buddhist "theology" and mysticism are closer than their Christian counterparts,[41] it is a matter of experience that the distinction between saṃsāra and nirvāṇa hardens into dualism. The popular view of Buddhism in China, for instance, is that it is world-denying.[42] The mystics, then, restore the balance: the bodhisattva re-enters the city with bliss-bestowing hands, and the mahāsiddha sports in the diamond realm. But, they have not regressed to pre-Axial monism: they have seen the First Noble Truth, and transfigured it.

Harry Hay claims that gays think differently from straights because we think subject-to-subject, whereas straights think subject-to-object. Gays have "the gift of *analogue consciousness* by which we perceive the world through the gay window of subject-to-subject consciousness."[43] Well, maybe it's not quite so simple,[44] but I believe I have amassed enough evidence to show that it has, at least, been very difficult for the traditional religions, because of their heterosexual assumptions, to escape subject-to-object thinking. Therefore, I would like to work with Hay's claim that it is just at the point of subject-to-subject thinking that homosexuality is strong, and see what kind of a spirituality, within Buddhism and Christianity, can be built upon the assumption.

When two gay males relate erotically to each other as equals they affirm, first of all, their masculinity.[45] Neither is intrinsically "femme" or "butch," although these roles may be temporarily adopted in a playful manner. There is, then, the *similarity* of the partners, the presence of an analogue or subject-to-subject consciousness, in contrast to the familiar/mysterious, subject-to-object consciousness of heterosexual relations. This is a powerful image of non-duality—wisdom is in method as method is in wisdom—and of sanctification—God is in the human as the human is in God (cf. John 14:20). Secondly, in a homoerotic relationship of equals, there is no predetermined distinction, either in theory or practice, between active and passive roles, as there is, in theory, in heterosexual symbolism (a symbolism which is not, of course, carried out in heterosexual practice!). Because of this, there can be a partnership and the mutuality of friendship rather than the possession, domination, and control of a presumed weaker spouse or recipient.

As long as this structure is founded upon the Axial truths of (for Buddhism) the First Noble Truth and (for Christianity) God, and taught as something one comes to later in the path, after the Axial truths have been properly assimilated and our passions have become somewhat less enslaving, it will not be a regression to pre-Axial pro-cosmism, a mere importation of fairy doings *tout court*, but a taking refuge and a baptism at the levels of the bodhisattva, mahāsiddha, and saint. It will be not only the acceptance of the fairy vision, but the ennobling and the transfiguration of it.[46]

Such a grammar would be a translation into the mystical realm of the emerging political and social reality in which humans of either sex and any sexual preference are enabled to relate to each other in freedom, play, intimacy, and ecstasy.

> Meister Eckhart met a beautiful naked boy.... Who are you? "A king."... He led him to his cell. Take whichever coat you will. "Then I should be no king!" And he disappeared. For it was God himself— Who was having a bit of fun.[47]

¹ "Can Gays and Lesbians Come Out and Be Faithful Catholics?" Interview with Sister Jeannine Gramick, S.S.N.D., *U.S. Catholic* 57.8 (AUG 92): 6–13. The quotation is taken from page 8.

² This term is used by Judith Butler in *Gender Trouble: Feminism and the Subversion of Identity* (New York: Routledge, 1990). I am indebted to Professor Mary McClintock Fulkerson of Duke University Divinity School for this reference.

³ This Christian term for "creative re-writing of the standard explanatory system" does not seem to have an exact equivalent in other traditions. Thus, the debates between the Christian theologian John Cobb and the Zen philosopher Masao Abe have been officially called "theological encounters." In this essay I am assaying, for both Buddhism and Christianity, an exercise similar to that of Sally McFague who, in *Models of God: Theology for an Ecological, Nuclear Age* (Philadelphia, PA: Fortress Press, 1987), re-images the Christian God as Mother, Lover, and Friend.

⁴ The appropriateness of first- and second-person language, especially for discussions of sexuality, is argued by Carter Heyward in *Touching our Strength: The Erotic as Power and the Love of God* (San Francisco: Harper & Row, 1989). I would also note that the pioneers of objective science, such as Lavoisier, used "I" statements without embarrassment. The "it-was-observed" statement is a recent invention, and it needs to defend itself if it wishes to survive.

⁵ Evelyn Underhill proposes that spiritual marriage is a symbolism preferred by "...the mystic for whom intimate and personal communion has been the mode under which he best apprehended Reality," whereas "[t]he metaphysical mystic, for whom the Absolute is impersonal and transcendent, describes his final attainment of that Absolute as *deification*, or the utter transmutation of the self in God." *Mysticism* (London: Methuen, 1960, University Paperbacks reprint of the twelfth edition, London: Methuen, 1930), p. 415.

⁶ Jerome, Letter 22, "To Eustochium: The Virgin's Profession." Quoted from the Loeb translation in *Women and Religion: A Feminist Sourcebook of Christian Thought*, edited by Elizabeth Clark and Herbert Richardson (New York: Harper and Row, 1977), p. 60f.

⁷ *Life*, 29:13–14. *The Collected Works of St. Teresa of Avila*, translated by Kieran Kavanaugh, O.C.D. and Otilio Rodriguez, O.C.D. (Washington DC: Institute of Carmelite

Studies, 1976), vol. 1, p. 193f. The Vatican recently decreed that Teresa of Avila should be known as Teresa of Jesus, which was her name in religion.

8 A detail of this statue (unreferenced, however) is used on the cover of *The Collected Works*, volume 1. I am presuming that Teresa was heterosexual, since there appears to be no reason to doubt it.

9 *The Collected Works of St.John of the Cross*, translated by Kieran Kavanaugh, O.C.D. and Otilio Rodriguez, O.C.D. (Washington DC: Institute of Carmelite Studies, 1979), pp. 408–565, *passim.*

10 *Yab-yum* visualizations are restricted to the higher Tantras which are usually transmitted orally and thus not available to standard scholarly footnoting. The Kālacakra Tantra, however, is an exception—it is one of the highest Tantras, yet it is transmitted publicly and its *sādhana* (liturgy) and explanation have been published. For a reliable introduction, see *The Wheel of Time: The Kalachakra in Context* by Geshe Lhundup Sopa, Roger Jackson and John Newman (Madison WI: Deer Park Books, 1985). For text and commentary see *The Kālachakra Tantra: Rite of Initiation for the Stage of Generation* by Tenzin Gyatso (Dalai Lama XIV), translated by Jeffrey Hopkins (London: Wisdom Publications, 1985).

11 Note that this is opposite to the symbolism normally found in Hindu Tantra, where energy or power is female (*Śakti*). The emphasis on the superiority of the male may indeed be merely a peculiarity of the Sarma (New Translation) lineages of Tibetan Buddhism, about which most is known. Reliable material is just beginning to become available on the Nyingma (Old Translation) and Dzogchen (Great Perfection) traditions, in which, apparently, a *spontaneously arising* female energy (i.e., one that has no need to await male penetration) is dominant. See, for example, *The Sovereign All-Creating Mind, The Motherly Buddha*, translated by E.K. Neumaier-Dargyay (Albany NY: State University of New York Press, 1992). (In a personal communication, Professor Dargyay made the encouraging remark that my "reference to the gsar-ma view of tantric practice is very revealing.")

12 My late teacher, Richard H. Robinson, introduced us to the principles of Sanskrit grammar by means of the following limerick:

> There was a young lesbian of Khartoum
> Who invited another to her room.
> As she put out the light,

She said, "Let's get this right:
Who does what, and with what, and to whom?"
13 It might be objected that Theravāda maintains precisely this distinction. However, the prominent Theravādin teacher Buddhadāsa argues for the co-existence of saṃsāra and nirvāṇa while rejecting the charge that this makes him a crypto-Mahāyānist. See *Me and Mine: Selected Essays of Bhikkhu Buddhadāsa,* edited by Donald K. Swearer (Albany NY: State University of New York Press, 1989), especially essay 8, "Nibbāna Exists in Saṃsāra."
14 June Singer, *Androgyny: Toward a New Theory of Sexuality* (Garden City NY: Doubleday, 1976).
15 The term for this is either *nazar ilā'l-ahdāth* (Annemarie Schimmel, *Mystical Dimensions of Islam* [Chapel Hill: University of North Carolina Press, 1975], p. 290) or *nazar ilā'l-murd* (Hellmut Ritter, *Das Meer der Seele: Mensch, Welt und Gott in den Geschichten des Fariduddin 'Aṭṭār* [Leiden: Brill, 1955], p. 459). Professor Carl Ernst of the University of North Carolina at Chapel Hill, to whom I am indebted for the reference to Ritter, tells me that these terms are synonyms, literally meaning "looking at the youthful" and "looking at the beardless" (*murd* also meaning, when used of trees, "leafless," therefore, in general, "without anything sprouting out").
16 Sanā'ī, *ghazal* 161. Quoted in Julie Scott Meisami, *Medieval Persian Court Poetry* (Princeton NJ: Princeton University Press, 1987), p. 250f. I am indebted to Professor Carl Ernst for referring me to this book.
17 "The lovely youths addressed and extolled in the Persian *ghazal*...should not be construed as literal participants in a factual love affair...." Meisami, p. 251.
18 Meisami, p. 250.
19 Meisami, p. 249f.
20 Paul Veyne, "Homosexuality in Ancient Rome," *Western Sexuality: Practice and Precept in Past and Present Times,* edited by Philippe Ariès and André Béjin, translated by Anthony Forster (Oxford, England and New York, NY: Basil Blackwell, 1985), pp. 26–35.
21 Ihara Saikaku, *The Great Mirror of Male Love,* translated by Paul Gordon Schalow (Stanford CA: Stanford University Press, 1990), p. 28.
22 Veyne, p. 32. Meisami, p. 249. Schalow, p. 29.
23 Most sources attribute the use of the word fairy to the reading of W. Y. Evans Wentz, *The Fairy-Faith in Celtic Countries* (Gerrards Cross, Buckinghamshire, England: Colin Smythe Ltd., 1977; reprinted from the original 1911 Oxford

University Press edition, with a new foreword by Kathleen Raine), who uses the spelling *Faerie* (always capitalized) only when referring to Malory and Spenser. The uncapitalized form *faerie* is used occasionally by J.R.R. Tolkien in "On Fairy-Stories," *Tree and Leaf* (London: Unwin, 1964), pp. 12–70.

24 Margot Adler, *Drawing Down the Moon: Witches, Druids, Goddess-Worshippers, and Other Pagans in America Today* (Boston MA: Beacon Press, revised and expanded edition, 1986), chapter 12, "Radical Faeries and the Growth of Men's Spirituality." Mark Thompson, "This Gay Tribe: A Brief History of Fairies," *Gay Spirit: Myth and Meaning,* edited by Mark Thompson (New York: St. Martin's Press, 1987), pp. 260–278; see p. 268 for Thompson's objection to Adler's contention that fairies are a variety of neo-paganism. "Fairy" was suggested by Arthur Evans, in *Witchcraft and the Gay Counterculture: A Radical View of Western Civilization and Some of the People It Has Tried to Destroy* (Boston MA: Fag Rag Books, 1978) for a gay male who linked his sexuality with his spirituality, and Harry Hay is credited with activating, or politicizing, this spirituality by combining the words "radical" and "fairy." Thompson, p. 261, and Stuart Timmons, *The Trouble with Harry Hay: Founder of the Modern Gay Movement* (Boston MA: Alyson Publications, 1990), p. 250. I am indebted to Trebor, a fairy friend living in San Francisco, for the reference to Timmons.

25 I have not been to a gathering myself, but I have talked with fairies who have, particularly when I attended a radical fairy potluck in San Francisco on Saturday, August 22, 1992, where a home video of a gathering in Oregon was shown. There are accounts of "A Spiritual Conference for Radical Fairies" in the Arizona desert on Labor Day weekend, 1979, which may be taken as the founding gathering, in Thompson (pp. 269–278) and Timmons (pp. 265–268). "Mountains and Mist" by Mohanon in the gay journal *RFD* for Winter 1991 (issue 68), pp. 40–42, reports on a gathering in North Carolina between September 20 and 22, 1991.

26 Timmons, p. 252. "Genderfuck" usually refers to a person who wears a mixture of clothing items parodying both male and female attire at the same time.

27 For the importance of parody in gay lifestyles, see Butler, *Gender Trouble,* chapter 3, "Subversive Bodily Acts."

28 I then classify the Axial traditions along a spectrum from minimally anti-cosmic (e.g., Taoism) to maximally anti-cosmic (e.g., Jainism), but that is irrelevant to this essay.

29 James Broughton, "The Holiness of Sexuality," *RFD* 68 (Winter 1991): 43–46.

30 One of the four great vows, commonly recited in East Asian Mahāyāna, is: "Desires are inexhaustible: I vow to put an end to them." (Translation as used in the Zen Center of Los Angeles.)

31 John Welwood, *Journey of the Heart: Intimate Relationship and the Path of Love* (New York: HarperCollins, 1990).

32 In a personal communication, Professor Paul Schalow remarked that this sentence gave him pause since it "puts an awful burden on the participants if everything is intrinsic." However, from hearing Welwood talk about his book, I do not think that he wishes to emphasize the partners' *responsibility* for maintaining the relationship, but merely to point out how relationships may now be based on mutual love rather than on social or political expediency.

33 Welwood, p. 2. (Italics in original.)

34 Welwood, p. 21, note 1 under "Introduction."

35 G. Rattray Taylor, *Sex in History* (New York: Vanguard Press, 1970).

36 Taylor, index *sub* "Matrism" and "Patrism."

37 The possibility of living alone, without slaves, was inconceivable to the ancient Greeks. "When Athenaeus's 'Sophists at Sup' try to imagine life without slaves, they can only imagine a world in which utensils move automatically, bread bakes itself, and fish voluntarily season and baste themselves, flipping themselves over in the frying pan at the appropriate time."—Dale B. Martin, *Slavery as Salvation: The Metaphor of Slavery in Pauline Christianity* (New Haven: Yale University Press, 1990), footnote 168 to text on p. 42. The means of production were such that it could not occur to a freeborn male of the time that he himself might do the cooking.

38 Roger Corless, "The Christian Mystic as *paganus redevivus*: A Hermeneutical Suggestion," *The Merton Annual: Studies in Thomas Merton, Religion, Culture, Literature & Social Concerns,* edited by Robert E. Daggy, Patrick Hart, O.C.S.O., Dewey Weiss Kramer and Victor A. Kramer, vol. 3 (New York: AMS Press, 1990), pp. 203–216. (I have some misgivings about using the word "mystic" and its derivatives, but I can find no other convenient term for "one who takes a spiritual system seriously and reports experiential knowledge of its effectiveness.")

39 And I cannot even footnote it properly. It resided in the oral tradition when I was an undergraduate in the

Theological Faculty (American English: "Department") of King's College, University of London.

40 The opening lines of "God's Grandeur" by Gerard Manley Hopkins. *Gerard Manley Hopkins: Poetry and Prose*, selected and edited by W.H. Gardner (Harmondsworth, Middlesex, England: Penguin Books, 1953), p. 27.

41 It has therefore been suggested that the use of Buddhist "theology" in Christianity could heal the Christian split between the theologian and the mystic. John P. Keenan, *The Meaning of Christ: A Mahāyāna Theology* (Maryknoll NY: Orbis Books 1989).

42 Shiangtai Tuan, a computer scientist at Duke University, who was brought up in China, tells me that all he knew of Buddhism as a child was that, if you were serious about it, you didn't have sex, eat meat, or drink alcohol.

43 Thompson, p. 273. A peculiarly flaccid version of Hay's statement, lacking the arousing philosophical terms, is quoted in Timmons, p. 256.

44 And maybe it does not *begin* with analogue consciousness, but with dance. Ron Long, a respondent on the panel at which this essay was originally presented, remarked that the fairies begin with dancing, the body, working-out— "as we are in the world, so we are in our bodies." The priority of dance over theory would be consonant with my suggestion that fairy spirituality is pre-Axial. Joseph Campbell, in one of his PBS-TV interviews with Bill Moyers, told of a Christian minister who, having toured a number of Shinto shrines, complained that he did not understand Shinto theology. The Shinto priest replied: "I do not think we have a theology: we dance." This is illuminating, since I classify Shinto as a surviving pre-Axial system.

45 My description here ignores gayness as a range, and, for the sake of simplicity, focuses on a presumed ideal type of gay male relationship.

46 This, of course, is from the Buddhist and Christian perspectives. Perhaps I need to repeat that I am neither advocating nor disparaging pre-Axial or Axial systems. Their antithesis is a fact which, here, I am merely accepting. If you are entirely comfortable with being a fairy, and do not agree with the Axial teachings of Buddhism and Christianity, this essay will not speak to you.

47 Raymond Bernard Blakney, *Meister Eckhart: A Modern Translation* (New York: Harper and Row, 1941), p. 251. This vision is the basis for the icon "Holy Wisdom" by Robert Lentz, in which a third-world and somewhat androgynous young man is shown naked (but, as Mother

Julian might say, "all in seemly fashion"—we see nothing below the waist!) and holding the planet earth. The image fits remarkably well with my suggestion that the Christian mystic arises bearing Gaia transfigured. For information on this and other icons of Robert Lentz, contact Bridge Building Images, P.O. Box 1048, Burlington, VT 05402, telephone (802) 864-8346.

IV. Daniel T. Spencer:

Shattering the Image,
Reshaping the Body:
Toward Constructing a Liberating
Lesbian and Gay Ecclesiology

1. Introduction

Theology is our corporate reflection on God and
God's relation to the world, and is rooted in the contradictions we experience as individuals and communities between the convictions of our faith and our
actual lived experience. Theologies of liberation make
the further claim that this reflection must be rooted in
the experience of suffering of subjugated peoples and
groups, and in their efforts to resist domination and
oppression and bring about liberation.[1] Ecclesiology
is that branch of theological reflection that examines
the nature, shape, and identity of the church. It also is
forged, in part, by the contradictions we as faith
communities experience in trying to live out the
convictions of our faith. More than other fields of
theological reflection, our understanding of
ecclesiology is subject to being tested for the claims
we make against the reality we try to live out.

Perhaps nowhere in the contemporary church in
North America is the gap between what the churches
have said about themselves as a locus of God's love
and gift of life, and how they are actually experienced,
as wide as it is for lesbian and gay people. Our
participation in the church is characterized by the
profound contradictions we experience there. For far
too many of us, the church as it has been shaped by
attitudes of homophobia and structures of heterosexism has been a community of oppression rather than

liberation. This experience causes us to raise critical questions about the nature of the church and to search for an understanding of the church that is liberating for us.

This search is a profoundly personal and corporate task. It is personal, because it begins and is rooted in our individual journeys as lesbians and gay men, often in isolation from each other, to discover what it means to affirm our identity as both Christian and gay. It is corporate, because as we begin to discover each other, we experience a liberating dimension to the communities we begin to shape that goes beyond the sum of our individual experiences. This search for a new understanding of church is also in communion with other communities of faith: it draws on the broad range of experiences of historical and contemporary Christian faith communities while recognizing the importance of being rooted in the particularity of lesbian and gay experience.

It is this growing experience of church that I would like to reflect on in this paper. These reflections grow primarily out of my experiences in the lesbian and gay communities. Increasingly, bisexual and transgender people are talking about their particular histories, and their voices will have an impact on future ecclesiological reflection. I invite them and others to join in the discussion. For out of these experiences is emerging a new ecclesiology that challenges—but also invites—the churches to live as liberated communities of radical inclusiveness. Together we can reflect on the shape of this emerging lesbian and gay (L/G) faith community, and ask what challenges it poses to the broader church's understanding of itself, its ecclesiology.

a. Lesbian and Gay People and the Church:
the Contradictions

The search for a liberating understanding and experience of church begins and is shaped by the contradictions we experience as gay people. The contradictions between the teachings of the church that
shape our faith and our lived experience, arise parallel
to, and simultaneously with, our emerging identities
as gay or lesbian. One of the ways we experience
these contradictions is through homophobia—the
prejudice against, and fear, loathing, and hatred of
homosexual persons—both in the wider society and
especially within the church itself.

Many of us grew up in the church, and experienced it as a place of nurture, healing and redemp-
tion—until we realized our gay identities. At that
point we were faced with two primary choices: either
remain closeted, hiding our true identities from the
rest of the church family and increasingly experience
the world through a dualistic, split existence, or come
out as gay or lesbian and face hostility and expulsion
from the church. Either path left us wounded and
divided, often with no community in which to
integrate these two fundamental parts of our identity:
being gay and being Christian. The costs of either
path are high: the internalized homophobia and self-
hatred bred by the closet or coming out and risking
the alienation and isolation of being cut off from the
communities that nurtured and shaped us.

Like other subjugated peoples, this basic contradiction between our faith that God is a God of love
and compassion and our experience of hatred and
contempt from the church and society has caused us
to cry out, "How Long, God??" Why do we experience so much pain, suffering, confusion, and hatred,
and how long until we are simply accepted and loved
for who we are? Why is the very community that
names you central to their faith the one that drives us

away, the source of our pain? Where do we go and what do we do to experience your love?

These and other existential questions and cries emerge from a deep spiritual crisis and journey that many of us undergo while trying to reconcile these two seemingly irreconcilable parts to ourselves. At least initially, we often try to find validation from nongay people, and our approach to the church is usually apologetic: "Please let us in, we're just like you." Yet we are not just like them. Our experience has shaped us differently. Eventually we start to realize that we need each other to begin to name this difference, and reflect together on what difference it makes in our faith experience. Often this is a slow, halting journey of realization. We may connect with sympathetic and supportive nongay people, and think that this is enough. For some it may be. For most of us, however, it becomes a matter of survival and spiritual health to find others who name their reality and faith in similar ways.

This need for communities of wholeness, where we can affirm and are affirmed in our identity as gay and Christian, has led to an emerging L/G experience of church that differs from the dominant church. The emerging ecclesiology of this L/G faith experience is shaped both by the contradictions we have experienced in heterosexist churches and society, and by the constructive resources of joy and celebration, survival and thriving, we birth and nurture in our own communities. It is an experience and understanding of church rooted in the liberating efforts of L/G communities, to *resist* the oppression of heterosexism and homophobia and to *celebrate* our identity and uniqueness as a L/G people. It is an ecclesiology that locates the identity of the church in the move *from* the margins of community to the margins *as* community.

b. A Methodology for an Emerging Lesbian and Gay Ecclesiology

A liberating L/G ecclesiology consists of three intersecting moments:

(1) *Shattering the Image: Contradictions of a Heterosexist Church:* The first moment must shatter the image[2] that a heterosexist church can be the locus of God's love, justice and compassion. A L/G ecclesiology therefore begins with a social analysis of the reality of homophobia and heterosexism in church and society as a fundamental contradiction of the message of the Christian Gospel.

(2) *[Re]Grouping: Once You Were No People: The Formation of Lesbian and Gay Communities and Identities:* A primary source for a L/G ecclesiology is the experience of lesbian, gay, and bisexual people in forming our communities and identities in resistance to heterosexist oppression. From being "no people," hidden and closeted, we have emerged to create strong and vibrant communities that nurture our hopes and struggles for liberation.

(3) *Reshaping: Now You Are God's People: Marks of an Emerging Lesbian and Gay Ecclesiology:* The new experience and understanding of church that emerges from the experience of lesbian and gay people of faith is shaped by distinctive features or "marks." This ecclesiology in turn challenges the whole church to reshape its self-identity in response to the Gospel demands of justice for all people.

2. The One and the Many: Universality and Particularity

Before proceeding, is it valid to ask why develop a specifically lesbian and gay ecclesiology? Does this not violate from the beginning one of the traditional marks of the church, the church as catholic or universal, where all people experience God's love without distinction? At the simplest level, I would respond that a L/G understanding of church is necessary precisely because traditionally we have been excluded, ignored, and repressed *for being gay.* Our experience as gay or lesbian people has not been taken into account in understanding universality. The church universal has not been universal at all, but rather a "church particular," informed and structured to reflect a particular set of experience, usually that of white, heterosexual, and economically-privileged men. This particular church has been imposed on those of us whose experience is different and has been maintained and justified in turn through an ideology of universality.

In contrast to this assumed universality, with other feminist and liberation theologians I would argue that we move toward true universality not by ignoring our differences and the particular nature of all human experience, but by moving deeply into our particularities while listening to and being accountable to the claims and experience of other subjugated peoples. Liberation theologians pay attention to differences in human experience not for the sake of difference itself, but because these differences are turned into social inequalities based on race, gender, sexuality, and a whole host of other categories, and are used by dominant sectors to justify oppression.

In addition, as the African-American Liberation Theologian James Cone reminds us, the experience of God as "the transcendent can be encountered only in the particularity of a human situation."[3] A distorted universality based on oppression can hide God's presence. We who are gay or lesbian need a space apart from the constant oppression of the broader church to begin to understand and name the particularity of *our* encounter with the transcendent. It is out of that space that we will find the liberating resources that enable us to affirm God's presence with us.

3. Shattering the Image: Contradictions of a Heterosexist Church

a. Homophobia and Heterosexism: Rooted in the Dualisms of Patriarchy

The oppression of lesbians and gay men stems from structures and attitudes of compulsory heterosexuality, the tool of social control that mandates that all expressions of sexuality be channeled through patriarchal, heterosexual patterns.[4] Homophobia—the irrational fear and hatred of lesbians and gay men, and of homosexual behavior—operates with societal and religious sanction to keep heterosexism—the structuring of society to value and favor heterosexual men and their procreative sexuality[5]—in place.

Feminists and gay men insist that lesbian and gay oppression must be understood within the broader framework of patriarchal sexism: "Gay oppression is part of the very fabric of our society, reinforcing both male socialization to fear homosexuality and female socialization to remain passively attached to a traditional dominant male. This combination of homophobia and sexism is the very core of heterosexism."[6] As a part of sexism, heterosexism "maintains the subservience of women to men by punishing homosexuality and any deviance from the currently accepted range of masculine and feminine heterosexual roles."[7] Homophobia and heterosexism are the result of anti-body and anti-sexual attitudes and dualisms that pervade traditional Christian theology and teaching, and have in turn shaped Western attitudes and society structures. These anti-body dualisms intersect with the fundamental patriarchal male-female dualism to provide patriarchal societies with a powerful and pervasive method of control over anything and anyone designated as "other."[8]

b. *The Nature of Lesbian and Gay Oppression*

Homophobia and heterosexism combine to shape the distinctive nature of L/G oppression, characterized by both its internalized and externalized forms. Like the African-American experience of slavery, "the first and primary fragment of gay historical experience is that of oppression, and even of legalized genocide, on the part of both church and state."9 Whether it is the burning and hanging of homosexuals throughout medieval Europe or genocide of tens of thousands of gay men and lesbians in the Nazi death camps (only to have the gay survivors reincarcerated by the four "liberating" Allied armies for their "crime" of homosexuality),10 L/G history and identity is shaped by collusion of church and state in our oppression.

Unlike many other subjugated groups, this collusion continues openly today in the United States where lesbian and gay oppression is both religiously sanctioned and legally encouraged. Over half the states retain legislation that considers homosexuals and homosexual behavior criminal, a legal opinion most recently upheld by the Supreme Court in the 1986 *Bowers* v. *Hardwick* case. As a result of this historical and contemporary hostility, most lesbians and gay men have had two options: move deeper into the closet and remain isolated from each other, or cut oneself off from one's past and move into the urban "gay ghettos" of the large cities to look for community and acceptance from other lesbians and gay men.

Oppression of lesbian and gay people begins internally, often long before the person makes any public expression of her or his sexuality. Growing up in a society pervaded by hostile anti-gay attitudes, this oppression leads to self-denial and self-hatred, religious doubt and the consequent guilt and sense of unworthiness, loneliness and isolation, and fear of disclosure. Once one becomes identifiable as gay, the oppression broadens. Many openly gay men and lesbians face loss of jobs, housing, insurance rights.

and legal rights. Many are cut off from their families
of origin (including inheritance rights), expelled from
their churches, ostracized from their communities.
Gay men and lesbians lack both social and legal support for their relationships, and often are cut off legally from their children (from previous heterosexual
relationships). Anti-gay violence and harassment is
on the rise in the United States; currently only six
states include sexual orientation as a category in their
civil rights legislation.

Oppression of gay men and lesbians is mirrored
in and sanctioned by most of the mainline Protestant
denominations, Evangelical churches, and the Roman
Catholic church. We are denied ordination unless we
agree to hypocritical oaths of life-long sexual
abstinence and silence about our identity. The
churches refuse to bless our relationships and instead
denounce them as sinful and unnatural. In some
cases churches have refused baptism to children of
gay or lesbian parents. While some churches have
responded with compassion to the AIDS epidemic,
many others have responded with judgment and
blaming the victim. Few claim any responsibility for
the role the church's anti-sexual and anti-gay heritage
has played in bringing about and aggravating this
crisis through the virulent combination of homophobia with "AIDS-phobia." The church's unrelenting
hostility and negative attitudes towards homosexuality in general, and self-identified lesbians and gay
men in particular, have forced many gay people "into
exile," either out of the churches altogether or at the
margins.[11] What Rosemary Ruether says about the
churches in relation to women is also true for gay
men and lesbians:

> [T]heir power [is] so negative, that atten-
> dance at their fonts poisons our souls.
> They have become all too often occasions
> of sin rather than redemption, places

where we leave angry and frustrated rather than enlightened and healed.[12]

c. Shaking the Dust from Our Feet: Confronting the Church with the Crime of Sodom:

Theologically, the first part of a liberating L/G Ecclesiology consists in confronting the Church with the true crime of Sodom and Gomorrah: inhospitality and violence to those who bring God's message (cf. *Genesis* 19:1-29, *Matthew* 10:1-15). As did the first disciples, we come bringing a message of peace and liberation to our communities and churches; also like the first disciples too often the response we receive is not one of welcome, but of scorn and derision. Jesus's words to his disciples are words to us, as well: "If anyone will not welcome you or listen to your words, shake off the dust from your feet as you leave that house or town. Truly I tell you, it will be more tolerable for the land of Sodom and Gomorrah on the day of judgment than for that town." Shaking the dust from our feet by forming authentic L/G faith communities serves to confront the wider Church with its ongoing commission and repetition of the crime of Sodom.

d. Why Stay?

Given the history and pervasive nature of anti-lesbian and gay oppression in the church, why do we stay? Why bother with a L/G ecclesiology? Many of us, indeed, have chosen to leave and now have nothing to do with the church. For those of us who have stayed, the reasons why are as complex and varied as each individual. For many of us the church has been home, where we were first nurtured in the Christian faith and where we first found meaning and answer to our existential questions and spiritual journeys. Others for whom the church has not been home, still recognize that the Judeo-Christian tradition has provided the framework that shapes religious meaning in our lives.[13] For some it is a way to keep a connection with families and communities of origin. For others it is the conviction that social change happens through the transformation of existing oppressive institutions such as the church; that withdrawal of support alone is not sufficient. For these and other reasons, many L/G people have chosen to stay connected to the church, challenging its heterosexist nature in order to transform it.

4. [Re]Grouping: Once You Were No People: The Formation of Lesbian and Gay Communities and Identities

A liberating L/G ecclesiology claims as a primary source and authority the experience of lesbians and gay men in resisting gay oppression and working to transform our lives. This experience of church is rooted in our communities and identities. It recognizes that "being gay is far more than just a matter of sexual behavior; it is rather a whole mode of being-in-the-world."[14] Homosexual *behavior* has always existed, but it is only in the last 100 years in the West that the social conditions have existed for the formation of lesbian and gay *identities* rooted in L/G communities.[15] Since the mass mobilization of women and men during World War II first brought large numbers of lesbians and gay men together in U.S. cities[16] and particularly since the Stonewall riots in New York in 1969, gay men and lesbians have gathered in urban environments to create and sustain our own communities. The identities forged in these communities serve as the source for our emerging ecclesiology.

A similar process of forging new identities is occurring with lesbians and gay men who have chosen to remain within the church. A variety of paths and styles have followed. Here the experience of the African-American church is most helpful in articulating the different sociological and theological responses available to church-sanctioned oppression.

a. Invisibility

Like African slaves in the south whose oppression forced them to create a clandestine "Invisible Institution" as a means of celebrating God's presence in their resistance to slavery, the first experience of gay men and lesbians in the church has been a *forced invisibility*. Like the African slaves, our full humanity has been questioned and denied explicitly on theological grounds. While I know of no documentation of a parallel lesbian and gay "invisible institution" in the churches, the phenomenon it represents, of being forced to meet together clandestinely without the knowledge of the oppressor, has long taken place and continues to take place in many churches. Our need for and options for invisibility are different from that of the African slaves, but the effect is similar: oppressed peoples remaining in churches controlled by those who oppress them but refusing to allow the oppressors to name their theology and identity.

b. Forced Separation

In Los Angeles in 1968, Pentecostal pastor Troy Perry began the Universal Fellowship of Metropolitan Community Churches (MCC), a gay- and lesbian-identified Christian denomination. Like the independent black churches, MCC began as a sociological and theological response to the anti-gay discrimination practiced by churches in the United States. In his autobiography Perry explains that he does not believe there should be a segregated church for lesbian and gay people, but given the reality of gay oppression at this time it was necessary to find a space where lesbians and gay men "would have a place to worship God in dignity, and not as lepers and outcasts, but as His [*sic*] creation, as His [*sic*] children."[17] Like the Black Church in the African-American community, UFMCC is the one religious institution owned and controlled by lesbian and gay people.

c. Integration

Unlike the Black Church, the large majority of reli-giously-active gay men and lesbians remain in main-line Protestant, Evangelical, and Roman Catholic churches controlled by heterosexually-identified[18] persons. Although most remain closeted, some have chosen to leave the closet and challenge their churches from within by forming gay- and lesbian-identified caucuses and concerns groups. Examples of these include *Dignity* (Roman Catholic), *Lutherans Concerned* (Lutheran), *Integrity* (Episcopalian), *Presbyterians for Lesbian and Gay Concerns*, *Affirmation* (Methodist), and *Evangelicals Concerned.*

d. Integration and Separation: Lesbian and Gay Congregations in Mainline Denominations

In a trend that has developed in just the past few years, some gay- and lesbian-identified congregations are either forming in or choosing to affiliate with mainline denominations. These churches maintain autonomous lesbian and gay space for their congregational life while staying connected to their historic church traditions. Examples include Spirit of the Lakes Ecumenical Community Church in

Minnesota and Peace Church in Oakland, both affili-
ated with the United Church of Christ.[19]

e. Independent Congregations

There are also increasingly gay- and lesbian-identified congregations that are and have chosen to remain
independent of any denominational affiliation. An
example is Spirit of the River in New York, which has
explored affiliation with both the United Church of
Christ and the Christian Church (Disciples of Christ),
but for the time being has chosen to remain
independent.
 Given the current historical context and the
rapidly changing nature of the debate on lesbians and
gay men in the church, each of these expressions of
L/G church responds to a different set of conditions
and theologies, and each contributes to an emerging
L/G ecclesiology. This diversity of responses
strengthens the *ecclesia* of lesbians and gay men.
With this brief overview, we turn now to identifying
some of the distinctive marks of a L/G ecclesiology.

5. Reshaping: Now You Are God's People: Marks of an Emerging Lesbian and Gay Ecclesiology

a. Rooted in the Particularity of Lesbian and Gay Experience

The starting point for understanding the *ecclesia* of
lesbians and gay men is understanding and naming
the distinctive nature of L/G experience. The task of
self-identification is critical to the liberation of subjugated groups and peoples. For L/G people, this
includes claiming our personal and communal histories, and reclaiming our history from the distortions
and mystifications of the dominant heterosexist per-

spective that renders us invisible or inferior. This process of reclaiming the particularity of our experience is key not only to gain our sense of identity and validation, it also provides us with the energy and empowerment that our efforts at liberation require.[20] Being rooted in the particularities of our experience as gay men and lesbians therefore grounds a L/G ecclesiology.

At the same time we must avoid universalizing any particular gay or lesbian experience. Like gender, sexuality cuts across every other form of difference such as race, class, physical ability and age. In addition to our sexuality, all of us have identities developed by multiple factors that shape our experience and inform our perspectives. For a L/G ecclesiology to be liberating, it must recognize its partial, fragmented and incomplete nature, and be sensitive to the power dynamics present in other contradictions within our communities.

b. Location at the Margins

The *ecclesia* of lesbians and gay men will be a community at the margins: of the society, of the broader church, of our communities and families of origin. Gay men and lesbians typically find ourselves at the margins of whatever other community to which we belong, whether these are communities shaped by our racial and ethnic identity, by our class location, or by our religious affiliation. In contrast to other oppressed groups such as African-Americans and the poor in Latin America, claiming the particularity of our identity as lesbian or gay often cuts us off from our communities of origin that might otherwise serve as liberating sources in our struggles. We cannot simply return to our roots for sources of liberation, but must forge new sources from the communities we create.

Because of this, many lesbians and gay men of faith have resonated with John Fortunato when he likens our faith journeys in the church to that of exile, of being placed on the very margins of communities from which we expect nurture and life.[21] Others have used the analogy of a community of urban refugees, since many of us have felt forced to leave our places of origin to seek community in large cities, hoping to find some shelter from anti-gay hostility.[22] Our emerging experience and understanding of church recognizes the need to provide faith communities that allow space both to grieve our losses, as well as "embrace our exile" to discover the resources that come from life at the margins. Like the Latin American base communities and the African-American slave church, a L/G ecclesiology will recognize the power that comes from life at the margins, without romanticizing the cost of power-lessness.

c. Primary Accountability to Lesbian and Gay People

This L/G ecclesiology is accountable first and fore-most to its own people: the *ecclesia* of lesbians and gay men involved in the struggle for liberation. We also seek connection and accountability to the broader church, but only insofar as this fosters rather than blocks our efforts for justice and liberation. A L/G ecclesiology understands itself to be accountable also to the larger lesbian and gay community and to the diversity of lesbian and gay people and identities within our communities. This experience of church takes seriously the nature of the variety of differences between and among us. A L/G ecclesiology wel-comes all lesbian- and gay-identified and affirming persons, while also recognizing and affirming the need at times for gay- and/or lesbian-only space.

d. Liberating Sources for a Lesbian and Gay Ecclesiology

In addition to traditional Christian sources, a L/G ecclesiology makes use of three primary sources to shape its understanding of mission as the praxis of liberation: (1) the historical experience of resistance and struggle by lesbians and gay men, (2) spiritual and cultural resources located in contemporary lesbian and gay experience, and (3) analytical tools of power relations to identify and root out heterosexist structures.

In recovering and reclaiming our historical heritage, gay men and lesbians have gained and continue to gain from feminist attempts to recover women's histories. Although, in contrast to gay people, women have been continuously visible and identifiable through time, like lesbians and gay men they usually have been written out of history. Feminist historical analysis has developed methods to locate and make available to women historical sources of women's experience. These sources build a heritage of women's resistance and struggle that empowers current communities of women through liturgy and reflection. A L/G ecclesiology needs similar tools to develop liberating historical memories and sources for our own liturgy and empowerment.

A key resource for the *ecclesia* of lesbians and gay men is challenging mind/body and male/female dualisms. A L/G ecclesiology is an embodied understanding and experience of church, one that integrates sexuality and spirituality at its very heart. Through it we challenge the wider church to reexamine and renounce its anti-sexual traditions and teachings. It is an understanding of church that heals bodies shattered by sexism and heterosexism, as it heals its own body. In this we can draw on many experiences, especially the experience of the remarkable compassion and resiliency the L/G community has demonstrated in healing responses to the devastation of AIDS.

This emerging L/G church grounds its efforts at liberation in analyses of power that expose oppressive structures and practices at all levels. Starting from the particularity of challenging heterosexism and homophobia, the analysis and praxis seek to understand and stand in solidarity with other communities in struggle. Like the relation of Black Theology to the Black Church, a L/G ecclesiology needs a L/G liberation theology that is accountable to and serves as a self-critique of the L/G community and church. Many parts of our communities have internalized and continue to manifest oppressive dynamics of the dominant society. Critical to this process will be learning to confront privilege in our own communities that serves to oppress others.

e. Continuity and Discontinuity with Traditional Christian Sources

A L/G ecclesiology appropriates traditional Christian sources such as the Bible and theology through its commitment to liberation grounded in lesbian and gay experience. Like many women, lesbians and gay men experience the Bible as both liberating and oppressive. The thoroughly androcentric and often patriarchal and heterosexist nature of Scripture make its use as a liberating resource problematic for many gay people. As J. Michael Clark has concluded,

> [a] "closed canon" of scripture and a narrow, male-restricted ecclesiastical authority over doctrine and tradition have forced feminist theologians to reject even attempting to "read themselves into" accumulated, canonized (and hence closed) religious experience. Gay theology must do likewise....Our very

exclusion, whether as women or as gay people, becomes a criticism of scripture and tradition.[23]

A L/G understanding of church will appropriate those parts of the Bible and tradition that empower gay people while encouraging the community to construct its own sacred texts and scripture in which we find authority and meaning. Carter Heyward is helpful here in reminding us that scripture is holy and authoritative

> only insofar as we who read, study, preach, or teach it do so in a spirit of collaborative, critical inquiry steeped in collective struggle for radical mutuality between and among us all on the earth.[24]

Another way of saying this, is that authority lies in the community of praxis, not someplace outside from where it is imposed on us. For scripture to have authority, it must be grounded in our praxis of justice, healing, and liberation.

f. Features of the Ecclesia of Lesbians and Gay Men

(1) *Embodied:* Several features mark the *ecclesia* of gay men and lesbians. As mentioned before, it is an *embodied* community whose praxis heals the splits of anti-body and anti-sexuality dualisms. This understanding and experience of church emerges from a *liberating* as opposed to *liberal* understanding of community, one that is centered on the praxis of justice. Gathering for support as a lesbian and gay people is an integral and important part of this, but by itself it is not sufficient. L/G church must use this critical support to empower its resistance to gay op-

pression and struggle to transform society and the wider church. As the *ecclesia* of lesbians and gay men, we must embody precisely those liberating values and characteristics that are deemed antithetical to the dominant heterosexist sectors: a community of embodied same-gender and cross-gender relationships characterized by mutuality and reciprocity.

(2) Separation and Integration: The L/G faith community's response to a church whose stance and practice towards lesbians and gay men is one of pervasive abuse will have moments of both separation from and integration with the wider church. An adequate L/G ecclesiology must understand and be able to read the advantages and potential shortcomings of each. Moments of separation into autonomous gay and/or lesbian space are critical for affirming and deepening a L/G identity, and often frees up gay people for true worship and thanksgiving that may not be possible in integrated environments at this time. The danger of separation, however, is that it can lead to isolation and sectarianism. It can also in time lead to conservative tendencies, as separated communities eventually build up and acquire their own set of institutional privileges. Moments of integration lead to possibilities of ecumenism, connecting particularly with other communities of struggle. It also keeps clear and present the contradictions the community experiences, as the oppressor may be sitting in the pew next to you. The danger of integration without separation is in having to divert time and energy constantly to justify one's presence, and in eventually internalizing the hatred and abuse of the oppressor.

(3) Attention to Power and Authority: Because it emerges from an embodied community that seeks mutuality in relationships, a L/G ecclesiology will be

marked by attention to issues of power and authority. As in women's faith communities, our praxis will seek new understandings of power and authority, and new models of leadership. This is often difficult in practice, particularly in communities of women and men, for many of us have been socialized thoroughly in patriarchal models of leadership and relationship. As our faith communities grow and mature, considerable attention will need to be paid to the dangers of gaining access to power and privilege. There will be ongoing need for discerning power in mutuality, and paying attention to difference within the community.

g. Relation to the Wider Church: Reconciliation through Justice

The L/G ecclesiology sketched so far is not ideologically separatist, and therefore seeks to relate to the wider church. Such relations, however, must be shaped by a *non-apologetic* stance. We can no longer devote our energy and resources to trying to convince homophobic sectors of the church that we should be allowed in.[25] We *are* in. We *are* the church *now.* Our stance in a L/G ecclesiology is therefore *confessional* (this is how we experience God in our lives) and *invitational* (how do you experience God's presence?).[26]

Our faith communities seek to be a place of reconciliation with nongay sectors of the church. Here we combine Paul's understanding of justification by grace that sees the church as a place of reconciliation between previously alienated groups such as Jews and Gentiles, with the biblical commitment to liberation that maintains that true reconciliation takes place through justice. We affirm that true reconciliation and unity happen through our joint efforts to bring about justice through combatting homophobia and other forms of injustice. For this to happen, however, conversations with the wider church must be *power-sensitive.* We must recognize how our relations have been formed and structured along lines of oppression and privilege, and refuse to reproduce these dynamics. Dialogue is made possible only when we are clear where it is that our authority is located, and that that authority is respected in the interchange.

Finally, a L/G ecclesiology affirms the variety of forms the L/G church has taken with respect to heterosexually-identified churches, while calling each to ongoing examination of the benefits and risks of both separation and integration. At the same time we recognize that the choice of integration may not be ours, and so at the heart of L/G church identity is ongoing prophetic denunciation of the exclusive heterosexist nature of the wider church.

h. L/G Ecclesiology and the Traditional Marks of the True Church

With this overview of the distinctive marks of the *ecclesia* of lesbians and gay men, in what sense is it an expression of the true church of Jesus? Historically churches have sought to show that they incorporate the four traditional Christian marks of the Apostle's Creed: the true church is that which is "one, holy, catholic, and apostolic." While an extended exploration of the relation of L/G church to these four marks is not possible here, sketching some initial interpretations can help to flesh out further the distinctive contribution of our understanding and experience of being the church. As in the case of the other marks, a L/G liberationist hermeneutic grounded in the praxis of justice provides the key for relating the traditional marks to the *ecclesia* of lesbians and gay men. Rather than indicating simply the authenticity or inauthenticity of L/G *ecclesia's* claim to be the church, this justice interpretation of the traditional marks can give guidance to what extent we remain faithful to our calling as the church.

(1) One: The *ecclesia* of lesbians and gay men is marked by *unity* to the extent we participate in and invite other churches into the practice of justice. Grounded in the particularity of lesbian and gay experience, the *ecclesia* of lesbians and gay men calls attention to and invites others to join in the struggle against the concrete sins of homophobia and heterosexism, while joining others in justice struggles to transform whatever threatens life.

(2) Holy: The *ecclesia* of lesbians and gay men is marked by *holiness* to the extent we identify unconditionally with the mission of God in saying Yes to all that brings justice in life and No to all that unjustly threatens life. We understand and experience holiness from within the perspective of faith in our efforts to transform homophobic attitudes and practices, and heterosexist structures in church and society, understanding—as did the early church—that the persecution and suffering this generates is never justified, but may serve as indicators of our fidelity to practicing the reign of God.

(3) Catholic: The *ecclesia* of lesbians and gay men is *catholic* to the extent that we understands God's preferential love for us not as something we merit over others or keep within our community, but as an invitation to the whole church to abandon its search for God through alliances with oppressive forms of power. Our catholicity is found at the periphery in the experience of power in unalienated relationship rather than power through domination.

(4) Apostolic: The *ecclesia* of lesbians and gay men is *apostolic* to the extent that we remain evangelical in our identity, proclaiming and practicing with joy the reign of God in the particularity and concreteness

of lesbian and gay struggles for liberation in all its fullness. Marks of our apostolicity include the denunciation of homophobia and heterosexism as incompatible with the apostolic witness to the gospel of Jesus, inviting conversion to the gospel through renunciation of anti-gay attitudes and practices, and commitment to the liberation struggles of lesbians and gay men. L/G church is apostolic as well to the extent we reach out in solidarity to other churches in their struggles for justice, practicing mutuality in the sharing of our burdens.

In each case the traditional marks are given meaning and content through the practice of justice of lesbians and gay men, understood from the perspective of faith as practice of the reign of God.

6. *Conclusion*

To conclude, in reflecting on the *ecclesia* of lesbians and gay men, it is our resistance to oppression and our efforts to transform heterosexist structures and the celebration of God's presence in our communities that grounds an emerging L/G liberating ecclesiology. Such an understanding and experience of the church consists of three intersecting moments:
— Naming the sins of homophobia and heterosexism in order to shatter the image of a heterosexist church;
— Locating its source in the emerging communities of lesbians and gay men;
— Reshaping and revisioning the church through a distinctive ecclesiology grounded in the praxis of lesbian and gay people of faith.

The marks that distinguish a L/G ecclesiology include:
— the particularity of L/G experience as its starting point and primary source;

— its use of liberating sources rooted in historical and contemporary experiences of L/G praxis of liberation;

— critical appropriation of traditional Christian sources including scripture and theology from the standpoint of justice for gay people;

— emphasis on a liberating community with the praxis of justice as its center;

— relation to the broader church through a non-apologetic stance in hopes of reconciliation through justice;

— relation to the traditional marks of the church through a liberationist hermeneutic grounded in the praxis of justice.

The *ecclesia* of gay men and lesbians is part of the true church of Jesus to the extent its identity is grounded in proclaiming and practicing the reign of God in the liberation struggles of lesbians and gay men and all others who experience oppression. And—so is the rest of the church.

1 For the earliest claims of liberation theologians, see Gustavo Gutierrez, *A Theology of Liberation* (Maryknoll, NY: Orbis, 1973), pp. 6-15; and James Cone, *A Black Theology of Liberation* (Philadelphia & New York: Lippincott, 1970), esp. chapter 2.

2 Nelle Morton in *The Journey is Home* (Boston: Beacon Press, 1985) discusses the importance of not ignoring, but actively shattering the images that have been created and used to subjugate people.

3 James Cone, *Speaking the Truth: Ecumenism, Liberation, and Black Theology* (Grand Rapids, MI: Eerdmans, 1986), p. 115.

4 Beverly Wildung Harrison, "Misogyny and Homophobia: The Unexplored Connections," in *Making the Connections: Essays in Feminist Social Ethics,* Carol Robb, ed. (Boston: Beacon Press, 1985). See also Carter Heyward, *Our Passion For Justice: Images of Power, Sexuality, and Liberation.* (New York: Pilgrim Press, 1984), esp. chapters 5, 6, 11, and 22.

5 J. Michael Clark, *A Place to Start: Toward An Unapologetic Gay Liberation Theology* (Dallas: Monument Press, 1989), p. 30.

6 Ibid., p. 29.

7 G. Goodman et al., *No Turning Back: Lesbian and Gay Liberation in the '80s* (Philadelphia: New Society, 1983), p. 29; cited in Clark, *A Place to Start,* p. 29.

8 Harrison, *Making the Connections,* p. 136; Clark, *A Place to Start,* pp. 31-32. For an excellent exposition of the source and influence of dualisms on Christian theology and tradition, see James Nelson, *Embodiment: An Approach to Sexuality and Christian Theology* (Minneapolis: Augsburg, 1979).

9 Clark, *A Place to Start,* p. 25.

10 For the experience of gay men in the Nazi camps, see Richard Plant, *The Pink Triangle: The Nazi War Against Homosexuals* (New York: Henry Holt, 1986) and Heinz Heger, *The Men With the Pink Triangle* (Boston: Alyson Publications, 1980).

11 John Fortunato, *Embracing the Exile: Healing Journeys of Gay Christians* (New York: Seabury, 1982), pp. 14-16.

12 Rosemary Radford Ruether, *Women-Church: Theology and Practice of Feminist Liturgical Communities* (San Francisco: Harper and Row, 1985), p. 5.

13 Clark, *A Place to Start* p. 13.

[14] Ibid., p. 1.

[15] John D'Emilio, "Capitalism and Gay Identity," in *Powers of Desire: The Politics of Sexuality,* Ann Snitow, Christine Stansell, and Sharon Thompson, eds. (New York: Monthly Review Press, 1983), pp. 100-113.

[16] Allan Bérubé, "Marching to a Different Drummer: Lesbian and Gay GIs during World War II," ibid., pp. 88-99.

[17] Troy Perry, *The Lord is My Shepherd and He Knows I'm Gay* (Los Angeles: Nash Publishing, 1972), pp. 221-222.

[18] Many of these churches in fact have large numbers of homosexual persons, usually men, in leadership positions who wield a great deal of control. These church leaders are inevitably closeted, that is *heterosexually-identified,* rather than *gay-identified.* Because of the need to protect their positions of privilege, they are often homophobic and one of the primary obstacles to ridding the churches of homophobia and heterosexism.

[19] While this paper focuses specifically on Christian G/L Ecclesiology, it is important to note that similar developments are taking place among Jews, including several gay- and lesbian-identified synagogues, such as Congregation Bet Haverim in Atlanta.

[20] Clark, *A Place to Start,* p. 20.

[21] Fortunato, *Embracing the Exile,* pp. 17-18.

[22] The image of urban refugee comes from a conversation with the Rev. Dan Geslin, co-pastor of Spirit of the Lakes Ecumenical Community Church in Minneapolis, September, 1989.

[23] Clark, *A Place to Start,* pp. 22-23.

[24] Carter Heyward, *Touching Our Strength: The Erotic as Power and the Love of God* (San Francisco: Harper and Row, 1989), pp. 82-83.

[25] Heyward, *Our Passion For Justice,* pp. 3-4; Clark, *A Place to Start,* pp. 123-124.

[26] Morton, *The Journey is Home,* p. xxv.

V. Ronald E. Long:

A Gay Partisan Response

I am a gay widower. I have survived the death from AIDS of my first long-term lover, and have now "married"—for lack of a better term—another AIDS widower. Harold Kushner dedicates his book, *When Bad Things Happen to Good People*, to his son whose life made the book possible, and whose death made it necessary.[1] Likewise, I have found my theological voice in relation to Jim's life, illness, and death. As he approached his death, Jim increasingly met my "refusal to give up hope" with the charge that I was refusing to face facts. And, of course, neither one of us ever pressed the question of what I was actually hoping for. It was only after his death that I learned that, despite his interest, Jim had refrained from asking me what I really thought about such things as religion, God, and death for fear that this academic would only answer in the evasive, irrelevant jargon of an expert. His death left me with the challenge to begin to speak the truth as I saw it, to rise to articulate awareness of what in fact I did think, and to publish it in the public arena as simply and as clearly as I could.

It was in the process of beginning to write that it dawned on me that I was thinking and speaking not only with a gay accent, but in a gay dialect, with its unique idioms and slant on things. My being gay influenced not only the style, but the substance of my theological work. Coming out and caring for a lover dying from AIDS had left its mark, and it was this marked man who now theologized. Self-consciousness of myself as a "gay theologian" was not unmediated. At least I had become aware of the term through discovery of the Gay Men's Issues in

Religion Group of the American Academy of Religion and through reading works of that pioneer, J. Michael Clark.[2] Such was the crucible in which I learned to name myself—and thereby focus my work—as a gay theologian. While all truths are but particular perspectives on the truth, I am convinced that, if we theologize in fidelity to our "gayness," we will give voice to a wisdom that is meaningful for both the gay community and the world at large. But our universal relevance will be realized *only* as we are true to the full reality of our uniqueness as gay men in the age of AIDS. Unfortunately, the declaration now worn on tee-shirts—"I can't even think straight"—is more of a "consummation devoutly to be wished" than a reality—especially among the theologically inclined.

1

I have written no memoir. But my work shares in that intellectual jockeying for position with respect to religious tradition that Susan Henking perceives in those texts she calls "AIDS memoirs." Her study constitutes an elegant argument—perhaps, it should be a reminder—that religions are what people do with them. Religious traditions live only as people use them to cope with the realities of their lives, and at the same time, understand their traditions in the light of the realities of their lives and times—with the result that both traditions and lives may be transformed in the process. The AIDS memoir, as a class, exemplifies this negotiation with tradition.

I believe it is helpful to recognize these transactions as "negotiations." Negotiations involve the art of compromise. Good negotiations result in compromises which compromise none of the interested parties. Settlements which result from either premature foreclosure or some form of betrayal represent the failure of the negotiating process. When the negotiation in question involves the interests of those directly affected by AIDS and our inherited religious traditions, the question whether the settlement represents an authentic or inauthentic compromise cannot be overlooked.

Henking concludes her paper with what seems to me a call for tolerance—and the suspension of the question of appropriateness. However, she here wears the mantle of "objective" academic observer, studying texts. The gay theologian in the age of AIDS, however, does not have the option of such an academic distance—but is by nature of his calling a partisan. The Enlightenment has taught us that religion must be judged in the light of the ethical. To be gay is to recognize one's homophilic and homo-erotic sensitivities as constitutive elements of self which are to be revered[3] unapologetically. If the theologian in part "tests the spirits" in the light of the ethical, so too the gay theologian must assess doctrines and spiritualities for their consonance with "gayspirit."[4]

2

Obviously, Hardy is not looking at all PLWAs ("persons living with AIDS") when he hails them as "prophets of an authentic spirituality." His prophets are those who have managed to recognize themselves in terms of the Christian mythos. In rallying around the insight that "God is love," they constitute a living rebuke to the hypocrisy of those who claim to follow Jesus, but who preach a "god of vengeance," instead of the loving Father of Jesus—and of those who profess that God is love but who live as if he were a god of vengeance. The prophetic office of these PLWAs lies not in the novelty of their vision, but in their fidelity to the vision of Jesus. Hardy also holds up this spirituality as authentic for the unchurched as well as the churched, and it is his advance of normative claims for his God-is-love spirituality that solicits my concern here.

While such a spirituality may be the spirituality of some PLWAs, I doubt that it can be a spirituality for the PWA ("person with AIDS") as such. Surely a spirituality for the PWA must help him deal with his disease. Since Hardy operates within the mythos of the agentic god of tradition, this involves a double movement—situating the disease in relation to God as well as the self in relation to the disease. To use Christian terms for the moment, surely the spiritual work of the PLWA involves a coming to terms with the disease as well as with his heavenly Father. Yet the juxtaposition of the reality of disease with the reality of God raises the issue of theodicy: if the disease is "sent" or even just tolerated by God, how can God be understood as love or even "Friend?" To know that the disease is not God's "punishment" does not help in knowing how it does stand in relation to God's "love." Faith that God is love baffles rather than marshals the spiritual resources to deal with the disease.

However we deal with the issue of theodicy,[5] inattention to the struggle the community has had with nomenclature overlooks what I find to be the really exemplary aspect of PLWA spirituality. The term "PLWA" was not ready–made; but had to be invented. Unlike "victim of AIDS" or "AIDS sufferer" of even "PWA," the self-designation PLWA allows the PLWA to see the disease as a facet of his life that must be integrated into the person's ongoing engagement with and in the world. AIDS brings with it shunning by the world and the temptation to withdraw from it. To know oneself as PLWA is to know that withdrawal is to be resisted and the world's shunning challenged. Quite simply put, to resist letting the disease mean death-in-life is spiritually more significant that sensing the embrace of a putative being called God. The knowledge of God as love simply does not imply or endorse, and thereby fails to marshal our spiritual resources for, such resistance.

Even as I suspect the God-is-love piety Hardy endorses is strangely irrelevant to the PLWA as PLWA, I am even more certain that it fails the gay as gay. Hardy knows that a spirituality valid for our time must transcend the dualism of the tradition, that which would separate soul and body as well as sexuality and spirituality. I will overlook Hardy's temptation to see contemporary integrations as "recoveries" and to see such "recovery" as a *fait d'accompli.* I would argue that the anthropology of Jesus nor of any biblical tradition is sufficient for our needs; and, like James Nelson, I can see the results of such a "sexual revolution" only in the future.[6] However, I do want to question more extensively here the claim that with Matthew Fox and André Guindon we have made such significant gains toward our needed integration of spirituality and sexuality in life and thought. My gay soul goes on alert when I read in Guindon that sex is the *language* of intimacy. Preference for the linguistic metaphor may signal residual dualism. And my suspicions are confirmed when sex is called the language of *intimacy.*[7] When theologians could no longer justify procreation as the exclusive justifiable "excuse" for sex, they began to substitute "intimacy" as that which alone justifies sex. Even our feminist colleagues fall prey to such temptation when they view sexuality as appropriate only within an antecedently established relationship.[8] Such an approach inhibits any real appreciation of "tricking" or forms of anonymous sex, except perhaps to name them poor substitutes for the real thing. Moreover, to read Guindon on tricking is to hear Augustine on sex in general: it seduces us into a life of self-loathing and renders us impotent for real love. In the fact of possible, indeed probable, addiction, best just to say "No!"[9] In my life, I have had too many truly good times in bathhouses and with people I picked up in bars, and too many of my fellow gays find "promiscuous" sex their exclusive sexual outlet—indeed, many by choice—to find such sexual "promiscuity" in and of itself so ethically and morally compromised and compromising. Guindon's tone indicates that he has failed to pursue what sex really means for gay men in the concreteness of their life as gay men, and has therefore not yet taken their embodiment as the passional beings they are with sufficient seriousness. No treatment of gay sex is adequate which has not yet fully discovered the legitimate satisfactions which a gay man can take from such sex. Without that, the analysis of sex in general remains suspect. Here especially the rest of the world stands to learn.

3

Roger Corless rightly perceives, it seems to me, the essential difficulty which gay men have in recognizing themselves fully in the light of our inherited Christian symbolic. He argues that the same is true of the Buddhist tradition. Gay men are thus forced to be spiritually innovative, "inventing" a spirituality true to their own fullness —a spirituality which, in turn, may prove a corrective to the traditions. I confess to some uncertainty as to whether Corless and I refer to the same thing by the word "spirituality." He obviously equates the mystical and the spiritual while I have always thought it meaningful to ask what the one has to do with the other. Let me, then, simply note what I mean by spirituality. A person's spirituality lies in his or her sense of direction and vocation in life—both individual and shared—the attempt to stay the course, and the style in which he or she does so. In this sense of the term, I share Corless' concern to develop a gay-specific spirituality.

Corless suggests, however, that gay specific wisdom may be brought to expression using Harry

Hay's notion or gay-specific subject-to-subject consciousness as its starting point. It is worth listening to Hay himself with regard to this idea. By 1975, Hay had become convinced that homosexuality was "a genetic means of high importance in preventing...disaster to the race."[10] He claims that, in 1976, it suddenly dawned on him that gays could generate such an effect through the sense of self and other that is specifically theirs. He recalls:

> In a letter, I was explaining how—when we thought about ourselves as preteenagers during the bleak years when we thought we were the only ones of our kind in the whole world—we would naturally be thinking about ourselves *as subjects.* And then, suddenly, when we *somehow* discovered that there *might* be another just like ourselves *somewhere,* and we started to think about him—and fantasize about—*him,* we would have been perceiving him in exactly the same way as we were perceiving ourselves. We would be perceiving him *as if* he were also subject. . . I had perceived my fantasy love as subject—*in exactly the same way as I perceived myself as subject,* in exactly the same way I had always perceived my teddy bear *as subject, in exactly the same way as I had always perceived the talking trees and the handsome heroes in my picture books as subjects.*[11]

Hay continues:

> Oh, I knew that all the other kids around
> me were thinking of girls as sex *objects*,
> to be manipulated—to be lied to in order
> to get them to give in—and to be
> otherwise treated with contempt (when the
> boys were together without them). And
> strangely, the girls seemed to think of the
> boys as objects, too.[12]

In Hay's fantasy, however,

> … he whom I would reach out in love to
> was indeed projected as being another
> me—*and the one thing we would not be
> doing* was making objects of each other.
> Just as in my dream (which I would go on
> having for years), he'd be standing just
> before dawn on a golden velvet
> hillside…he'd hold out his hand for me
> to catch hold of, and then we would run
> away to the top of the hill to see the
> sunrise, and we would never have to come
> back again because we would now have
> each other. We would share everything,
> and we'd always understand each other
> completely and forever![13]

What is salient to me is how romantic Hay's fantasy
is—and how sexless. His other self is a self like his
teddy bear and picture-book heroes. To be *subject*
does not require one to be sexed. As I recollect,
however, I did not fantasize so much about a prince
with whom I could run away to enjoy the sunrise, but
of a boy who would enjoy me indulging my desire to
explore his body, to know what he felt like—and who
would enjoy doing the same to me. My fantasy lover
was above all a male human animal, a friend yes, but
definitely a sexed body, indeed a boy who would

seem more male than I, and thus not just the same as
I at all. I would suggest, then, that, if there is a gay-
specific spirituality which can be gleaned from gay
experience, it is to be sought in the experience of
ourselves, not as mere subjects, but as embodied
persons. Indeed, we need to attend to our bodies to
discover what we as gay men know; we need to attend
to what we as gay men do with, as, and through our
bodies to begin to formulate a gay wisdom, even a
post-axial one. Harry Hay's Faeries dance, and so
does many another fairy. Perhaps John Fortunato's
friend is right, what we as gay men can do is to teach
the honky how to boogey.[14]

a. Many a gay man dances. And much of life in the
gay ghetto is taken up with activities that our culture
at large has relegated to the frivolous, not part of the
real business of life—partying, sex for the sake of
sex, even working out. Stereotypical gay activities are
frequently activities which are of the body. To be
sure, working out and dancing are not exclusively
gay, but persistence in them over the years may be
characteristically gay—for both HIV-positive and
HIV-negative, I might add. Is gay life but a prolonged
adolescence? Perhaps. But perhaps there is wisdom
here. It was someone wiser than I who said that we
must become as little children in order to enter the
Kingdom of God.

I have been both a professional dancer and a
body-building trainer. I have been struck by the
similarity of the postural requirements for graceful
movement and for safe lifting. Both require a strong
stomach, the contraction of which is centered between
the navel and the pubis (as for the yogis); the chest is
lifted, with the result that the neck is vulnerable and
the eyes lifted to behold the world and to meet others,
eye-to-eye and face-to-face. The upright posture
tends to become chronic among those who persist in
dancing or working out over time. While no one has

an ideal body, and perfect posture eludes us all, nevertheless it is such a postural ideal that we seem to "aim" at.

What are we to make of all this? First of all, ideal posture is the opposite of the fetal curl, the most protective of all bodily positions. This I remember from air raid drills when I was young and from coaching for civil rights demonstrations. To learn to walk upright is to dare to be vulnerable, but at the same time, to find ourselves at home in the world. Sam Keen once sounded the dictum, "As we are in our bodies, so we are in the world."[15] Perhaps the reverse is also true: As we are in the world, so we are in our bodies. To be at home in the world is to know oneself as a body in the world. What we are as persons may not be reducible to what we can say of our bodies. But, with Gabriel Marcel, I would argue that it is more appropriate to say that we are our bodies rather than we have bodies. And with him, I would argue that embodiment is not only a fact of our lives, but a vocation. We are summoned to be present in and through our bodies in the world.[16] But is this not the knowledge of our coming out as gay men, that it is important that our bodies stand for what we truly are, that we not be *poseurs—and* that we know who we are in terms of our passions and our cares? Perhaps, then, dancing and working out can be seen as the sacraments by which the sense of ourselves, made actual in that baptism which is our coming out, is reinforced and nurtured—that we are and are called to be bodies and embodied in the world.

b. If we are bodies in the world, we are also bodies among other bodies. As gay men in the world, we like to have sex with other gay men. We need study here. We need to explore the stuff of fantasy—in story, in dream and day-dream, and in erotica and pornography. We need to know how sex relates to fantasy. Most of all, we need to learn what stakes gay men have in sex, promiscuous and otherwise. What I am calling for is a phenomenology of sexual relations.

The phenomenological analysis of sex I am envisioning here would involve attention to the dynamics of consciousness during sex (and its foreplay) and of attraction.[17] Drew Leder[18] has called attention to the migratory character of consciousness. In everyday life, we normally attend to the world through our eyes and ears; thus our view onto the world tends to center our sense of ourselves in our head. But notice, when we strain to listen to something intently, we are apt to close our eyes and thus focus our experience of ourselves in our ears. We are still centered in the head, but differently. Suppose now, there has been a blackout, or simply that the light near the entrance way into our apartment has burned out and we have to walk some distance in the dark to turn on the nearest working light. Suppose further that earlier in the day we had rearranged the furniture in the apartment and that we must now make our way with care. In this circumstance, our consciousness is focused, not in our head, but in our hands and our feet as we step warily and feel for the light switch. Given this mobile nature of consciousness, how is it with sex? Most would agree that we come to identify with our bodies, that is, our consciousness of ourselves is as a body. But consider the bottom who cries out, "Fuck me! Fuck my hot ass!" What more is going on here? The bottom is not saying, "I like the feeling of something in my ass." If that were the case, he could have just as easily masturbated with a cucumber. Rather, he is focusing not on his own ass, but the thrusting dick. The thrusting dick is experienced, I would argue, as at once the other's and as his.

In order to appreciate this "merging" of self and other, we need to attend to the dynamics of attraction. Let us assume that this is a one-night stand—our lovers have just met at a bar and have gone home to have sex. Promiscuous or anonymous sex is *not* indiscriminate sex. It matters who touches us. While a certain glint in the eye or a smile may be that which seduces, it is other things that tend to be decisive in first attracting our attention. Gay men tend to be attracted by men who embody the characteristics of masculinity—from big dicks, broad shoulders and flat stomachs, to outright athletic prowess—perhaps youth to the mature and worldly *savoir faire* to the youthful. Many a businessman trusts in the attractiveness of the size of his wallet, while many an academic trusts himself to his large body of work. I would argue that we choose as our sexual partners those who can represent for us both masculinity and all other men. That is, men become attractive in virtue of their representative status.

Let us return to our pair. In the bottom's ecstasy, he is one with the fucking top—he participates vicariously in the perceived masculinity of his fucker, even as he knows himself attractive to his top. He then "knows" himself as both masculine and affirmed by his partner. And what's in it for the top? He, to, is for the moment focused in his dick, even as he enjoys the adulation his attractive bottom pays to his masculinity. What is at stake for both, then, is the masculinity of each as they bodily confirm and welcome one another as men. Such sex is important for those of us who grew up with a wounded sense of masculinity, who knew ourselves as essentially "different." We need to know we are "one of the boys"—and sex is the most compelling way to know our belongingness with other men, and perhaps to the world.[19]

Feminists among us, both gay and straight, may bristle at my suggestion. Suspicions are confirmed: gay men really aspire to know themselves one with the patriarchal powers. Yet I would argue that, if it is our masculinity that is affirmed in gay sex, it is an aberrant, deviant masculinity that is affirmed as masculine. Gays are no strangers to hierarchy, but hierarchical arrangements are merely provisional, not absolute. Today's top is tomorrow's bottom. Roles are interchangeable, pragmatic, not ontological. Roles are to be taken seriously, and with a grain of salt. (Here, I would suggest, is the root of high camp.)

What is miraculous is that the vehicle and symbol of group belonging—male bonding, if you will,—can *also* be the vehicle and symbol of intimacy. But, while sex can be the vehicle and symbol of intimacy, intimacy remains but one of the ends of sex. It all depends upon what we have "contracted" with one another.[20] But how can sex become the vehicle and symbol for intimacy? Sex requires the exposure of the privates. Good sex is a sign that the privates are attractive and enjoyable. Sex can also be the way of confirming the acceptability of those deeper aspects of myself, the truly private which is not visible when I drop my drawers. Intimacy is sex enacted at the level of metaphor. One can have meaningful and ethically justifiable sex without intimacy, even as sex is the metaphor for ideal intimacy. To use Guindon's linguistic metaphor for the moment, I would suggest that, if sex is a language, it is the language of meeting, not of intimacy. And intimacy itself is meeting in depth. Such a way of looking at things seems to accord with gay practice. Gay men sleep with one another because they enjoy sex with one another. Sex introduces us to another—and thus may be part of the search for a lover with whom we may decide (together) whether to have a monogamous relation or no. But I have suggested that sex is not just a matter of getting my rocks off, a sheer bodily activity. Sex is the sign, symbol, and vehicle[21] of our conviviality, whether intimate or no.

c. If we are bodies in the world, AIDS proves the body and ourselves to be mortal. The wisdom of the West has never been really good at helping us to understand and negotiate disease. We need wisdom. We need to explore the meanings of disease in general and of AIDS in particular, and to discern appropriate strategies for dealing with it. Work has begun. But more needs to be done.

In this connection, I cannot recommend Robert K. Murphy's book, *The Body Silent,*[22] highly enough. Murphy was an anthropologist at Columbia University who developed an inoperable tumor of the spine and died the slow death of progressive paralysis. His book is both memoir and study of life with paraplegia. He came to understand his disease as a metaphor for the human condition and therefore life reduced to its basics. And, although he came to experience his body as an alien substance, he nevertheless continued to speak of the struggle with the disease as a refusal to dis-embodiment from the world. A gay theology of embodiment stands to learn much from the memoir of this academic in how to understand AIDS.

d. Lastly, I propose we think about the dead, particularly since so many of my generation are no longer among us as bodies in the world. Norman Maclean concludes his novella, *A River Runs Through It,* with the following:

> Now nearly all those I loved and did not understand when I was young are dead, but I still reach out to them.
>
> Of course, now I am too old to be much of a fisherman, and now of course I usually fish the big waters alone.... I often do not start until the cool of the evening. Then in the Arctic half-light of the canyon, all existence fades to a being with my soul and memories and the sounds of the Big Blackfoot River and a four count rhythm and the hope that a fish will rise.
>
> Eventually, all things merge into one, and a river runs through it. The river was

cut by the world's great flood and runs
over rocks from the basement of time. On
some of the rocks are timeless raindrops.
Under the rocks are words, and some of
the words are theirs.
I am haunted by waters.[23]

The words under the rocks, these are the words of his
dead. In the movie of the same, the same words
conclude the film. Early in the film, moreover, it is
said that under the rocks, one might be able to hear
the voice of God. There is wisdom here. Memory of
the dead and the reality of God, these are interrelated.
Ancestral piety has long been ingredient in the
religious self-understanding of the human race.
Perhaps, then, we might follow the lead of Mary Hunt
in naming God as "friends,"[24] that is, God is the
communion of the society of friends, the living and
the dead, the communion of saints, and not a being
independent of this reality. Or shall we move in
another direction? In the early seventies, Corita Kent
and Joseph Pintauro came out with a number of small
books comprised of graphically displayed gnomic
sayings. One saying, in the spirit worthy of
Unamuno, has stayed with me over the years, that life
is a matter of getting so attached to everything that it
won't give you up.[25] Perhaps, then, we might see that
the refusal to give up the dead as dead, to refuse to let
them be of no account in the world, is one with our
vocation to resist that alienation from life in the world
which AIDS in particular seems both to impose and
solicit. Perhaps remembering the dead is a way of
protesting their disembodiment. Then our resistance
to the dis-embodiment which time brings might itself
be our oneness with a spirit we might want to call
God.[26]

4

I have gone on at some length responding to Corless
with a program of my own. My response to

Spencer's paper will be much shorter. Like Hardy, Spencer seems fundamentally comfortable with the Christian mythos as a gay man. Indeed, his traditionalism is evident in his passing remark that moments of separation may be important for freeing gay men and lesbians for "true worship and thanksgiving."[27] Salient is the sense that Christians *qua* Christians are called to worship and thanksgiving, rhetoric that has its roots in a piety towards a transcendent personal god. It is not identity, but community which is problematic in Spencer's paper. His paper is an attempt to order the ways self-consciously Christian gay and lesbian faith communities relate to mainline churches. My concern here is not with the particulars of the analysis or normative assertions. Rather, I am concerned, as a gay theologian, that Spencer's paper hides more than it discloses. In offering his study of Christian faith communities as "ecclesiology," Spencer has opted for one of the models of the church operative in Christian history. Unfortunately, in so doing, he conflates ecclesial reality with the "churches," those concrete communities which name themselves Christian communities or churches. To be sure, such faith community has meaning as a social context and support for the development of spirituality. However, I wonder whether such communities are the actual contexts in which full gay spiritual—indeed, gay Christian spiritual—formation takes place. Indeed, I would propose looking at the whole of the gay community itself as the fullest locus of gay faith/spiritual development. A *gay* ecclesiology needs to recognize the importance of the wider context of our spiritual life—our dances, our bars, our books, our support groups, to name but a few of the realities in terms of which our spirits are formed and nourished.

This leads me to make one final point in conclusion. Our academic work here is no mere academic exercise. We represent a community within the gay community trained to think about our life in ultimate perspective. Our forum provides the opportunity to propose, refine, and publish our efforts in this regard. But we need to be self-conscious about the fact that we are forming part of that context by which and in which future gays will be formed and informed. A recent TV movie pictured a family desperately trying to avoid coming to terms with the fact that the youngest son was gay.[28] Among the finals scenes is one in which the father, now reconciled that his son's gayness is a fact of life, asks his son, "What do you have to say to those who call homosexuality a sin and that you will be sent to hell?" The son is at a loss for words. The father responds, "We'll have to look into it. I don't want any son of mine to go out into the world defenseless." We are part of the process by which others like his son can be supplied a defense. But the best defense is a good offense. We cannot rest content with exposing the supposed hypocrisy of tradition or with exorcising the tradition of its homophobia. We must strive to give voice to a spirituality which we can uniquely discern. Then we can be of benefit to both our fellow gays and the world at large. It is not so much a matter of leaving behind monuments of our struggle with communities and traditions, but leaving behind testimonies to our refusal to be anything less than what we deeply and fully are. And that task is monumental indeed.

1 Harold S. Kushner, *When Bad Things Happen to Good People* (New York: Avon, 1981), p. 5.

2 See, especially, his *A Place to Start: Toward an Unapologetic Gay Liberation Theology* (Dallas: Monument Press, 1989) and *A Defiant Celebration: Theological Ethics & Gay Sexuality* (Garland, TX: Tangelwueld Press, 1990).

3 See Richard Goldstein, "Faith, Hope & Sodomy: Gay Liberation Embarks on a Vision Quest," *The Village Voice* 38.26 (June 29, 1993): esp. p. 29.

4 See the title of Mark Thompson, ed., *Gay Spirit: Myth and Meaning* (New York: St. Martin's Press, 1987).

5 For my own first attempt at working out a doctrine of God in the light of AIDS, see my contributions to Ronald E. Long & J. Michael Clark, *AIDS, God & Faith: Continuing the Dialogue on Constructing Gay Theology* (Las Colinas,TX: Monument Press, 1992). In that book, I seek not to characterize a divinity somehow antecedently known as the environing Other, but to define a notion of God that could commend itself to morally sensitive gay belief in the age of AIDS.

6 James B. Nelson, *Body Theology* (Louisville, KY: Westminster/John Knox Press, 1992), esp. pp. 15-28.

7 André Guindon, *The Sexual Creators: An Ethical Proposal for Concerned Christians* (Lanham, MD: University Press of America, 1986), *passim.*

8 See for example, Carter Heyward, *Touching Our Strength: The Erotic as Power and the Love of God* (San Francisco: Harper & Row, 1989), p. 7.

9 Guindon, pp. 177f. See also his characterization of bathhouse sex, ibid., p. 166.

10 Harry Hay, "A Separate People Whose Time has Come," in Thompson, ed., p. 285.

11 Ibid., p. 285f.

12 Ibid., p. 286.

13 Ibid.

14 John Fortunato, *AIDS: The Spiritual Dilemma* (San Francisco: Harper & Row, 1987), p. 82.

15 Sam Keen, *To a Dancing God* (New York: Harper & Row, 1970), p. 148.

16 See my discussion of Marcel's thought in Ronald Edwin Long, *Keeping Faith with the Dead: An Approach to*

Religion Through the Writings of Josiah Royce, Gabriel Marcel, and George Santayana, Columbia University Ph.D. dissertation. (Ann Arbor, MI: University Microfilms International, 1985), c. 3, esp. pp. 95-100.

[17] There is not a lot of spadework done here yet. Helpful to me has been Richard D. Mohr's comments in "Why Sex is Private" in his *Gays/Justice: A Study of Ethics, Society, and Law* (New York: Columbia University Press, 1988), pp. 100-106. He, in turn, is developing ideas suggested by the work of Murray S. Davis, *Smut: Erotic Reality/Obscene Ideology* (Chicago: University of Chicago Press, 1983). While Davis and Mohr both draw upon Thomas Nagel, "Sexual Perversion," *Journal of Philosophy* 66 (1969): 5-17 and Jean-Paul Sartre, *Being & Nothingness*, transl. Hazel Barnes (New York: Philosophical Library, 1956), pp. 382-407. Drew Leder's *The Absent Body* (Chicago: University of Chicago Press, 1990) is particularly helpful in providing the tools for an analysis of embodied consciousness. I know of no adequate treatment of the dynamics of attraction, but insights can be gleaned from C. A. Tripp, *The Homosexual Matrix*, 2nd ed. (New York: New American Library, 1987), esp. pp. 4-5.

[18] Leder, pp. 24-27.

[19] In and of itself, promiscuous sex is not morally problematic. Ethical questions arise in regards to how we treat our "tricks" (for example, do our actions compromise that basic friendliness I have suggested gay sex embodies?)—and as to whether our sex life is compulsive or not, foreclosing the option of developing intimacy should we choose.

[20] L. William Countryman is to be commended for his attempt to use an economic model of the exchange of goods in analyzing sexual interchanges. For a good example of his mode of ethical argumentation, see esp. pp. 250-259 of his *Dirt, Greed, and Sex: Sexual Ethics in the New Testament and their Implications for Today* (Philadelphia: Fortress Press, 1988).

[21] I owe this "trinity" of terms to James B. Nelson. See his *Embodiment: An Approach to Sexuality and Christian Theology* (Minneapolis: Augsburg, 1978), p. 18.

[22] Robert M. Murphy, *The Body Silent* (New York: W. W. Norton, 1990).

---

23 Norman Maclean, *A River Runs Through It and Other Stories* (Chicago: University of Chicago Press, 1976), p. 104.

24 Mary E. Hunt, *Fierce Tenderness: A Feminist Theology of Friendship* (New York: Crossroads, 1991), p. 104. I am not sure that she would be comfortable with my reductionist line of thought here.

25 Joseph Pintauro and Sister Mary Corita, *To Believe in God* (New York: Harper & Row, 1968), no pagination.

26 See Long, *AIDS,* pp. 14ff.

27 Dan Spencer, "Shattering the Image, Reshaping the Body: Toward Constructing a Liberating Lesbian and Gay Ecclesiology", see above in this volume, p. 102.

28 I cannot to date recall the title of the film.

Part B

Families and Coalitions:
Lesbians and Gay Men
Creating New Patterns of Community

I. Carter Heyward:

Embodying the Connections:
What Lesbians Can Learn from
Gay Men about Sex and
What Gay Men Must Learn from
Lesbians about Justice*

– in grateful memory of Karl Laubenstein –

1. Introduction

In this paper, I am wrestling with a double conundrum in which, I believe, lesbians and gay men live,
love, and work today in the U.S. First, in the context
of this sexually violent culture, which is the context of
all women's lives, whether or not we individually
have been sexually abused, can women honestly expect to be able to relate freely, or feel deeply, enough
to enjoy sexual play and pleasure as a sustained,
normative dimension of our sexual experience? Can
our gay brothers help us imagine participating in sex
play and pleasure for its own good sake in a world
such as ours?

The second part of the conundrum is this: In this
same social praxis—patriarchal, androcentric, sexist,
racist, and violent to its core[1]—what will gay men
gain, and what will they lose, to the extent that they
are actively resisting—standing and opposing—the
patriarchal, androcentric structures that shape dynamics of sexual violence against women, children, and,
frequently, gay men as well? Can we lesbians help
our gay brothers wrestle with what is required of
those who wish to stand with their sisters as pro-
feminist, pro-womanist, men actively resistant to
sexist, heterosexist, racist, classist patriarchy?

Put otherwise: First, what can we lesbians learn from many of our gay brothers—gay male culture—about *sex* that might literally open us more to deeply embodied sexual pleasure as a source of creative and liberating energy for loving ourselves, one another, and the world? *Second*, what *must* gay men learn from many lesbians—lesbian feminists—about justice that would strengthen men's commitment to the sexual well-being of women and children as a basic requisite for sexual pleasure to grow and thrive as a sustained, normative dimension of *men's*, as well as *women's*, sexual experience?

From a lesbian feminist perspective, the first of these possibilities is contingent upon the second. That is, we lesbians can trust *only* these lessons we learn about sex play and pleasure from those men whose lives, values, and commitments to women's well-being we trust. This contingency is clear to me as a lesbian feminist woman.

I propose also another contingency that is far more debatable among feminists: that is, that neither gay men nor anyone else—including lesbian women—should trust entirely those feminist voices that would suggest, or imply, that because women's bodies are so horribly the objects of sexual violence, we women must therefore live *necessarily* on the basis of our fear—our fear of sexual danger, our desire for sexual safety, and consequently a proliferation of sexual rules designed to keep us safe from unwanted touch, unwanted words, unwanted gestures, or unwanted fantasies directed at us.[2]

My effort in this paper is surely not to suggest that the sexual danger in which we live is not real, pervasive, and necessarily of intense, immediate concern to all women and men, lesbian, gay, bisexual, and heterosexual, of all colors, cultures, and classes who are in touch with reality. Rather, my experiential and intellectual, moral and political, hunch is that a way to reckon with sexual danger that will keep us safer, finally, than by tightening up our rules, our psyches, and, if we are women, our cunts, *is to learn together how to challenge sexual violence at its patriarchal, androcentric, and, in our cultural place, racist and capitalist, root.* This is the primary purpose of this exploratory paper.

While we cannot do without standards, guidelines and principles to help us do one another as little harm as possible in our work and love, we can, I believe, learn how to be more communal, more imaginative, and basically more courageous in matters sexual and, thereby, how to live more genuinely *ethical* lives: that is, bound less by fear and rules and more by a commitment to helping generate conditions for right—mutually-empowering—relation in our bedrooms, classrooms, offices, workplaces, play places, private and public places. I believe we can learn how to sit more lightly with rules by taking more seriously our capacity as moral agents. As Sara Lucia Hoagland writes, "Much of what is called 'ethics' in our culture involves not the integrity and moral capability of an individual, but rather the extent to which she participates in the structural hierarchy of a social group or organization by adhering to its rules."[3] But we cannot learn to be genuinely ethical, moral, alone. We need one another's teaching, learning, and accountability.

In order for patriarchal violence to be challenged and diminished, men must learn to be accountable to women's well-being in men's sexual practices and development. This is true of gay men as well as bisexual and heterosexual men, for *all* men's sexual attitudes and practices are connected to how they experience themselves as men and how they experience other men and women. *All* men, and women, are shaped to some degree by a sexist construction of women.

I *know* that gay men need to hear and take to heart what many lesbians have been learning about justice, violence, and liberation. I *believe* also that lesbians need to learn something from gay men about sex, bodies, and pleasure. I believe we need to learn this in order not only to inspire our sexual play and pleasure, but also to spark our capacities to live fully as moral agents, subjects of our lives, rather than as *de-moralized*[4] women embroiled in struggles for justice of many forms but, in the midst of it all, afraid of our *body-selves,* the root of our creative power, and not very open much of the time—physically, mentally, or intellectually—to full-bodied sexual pleasure—an experience of coming into our power.

2. *Challenging Sexual Violence at Its Root*

Patriarchy is a social system of domination and control. Racist capitalist patriarchy, which is where we are, is a system in which privileged white males historically have valued themselves, other white males, and all other people, creatures, and resources according to the amount of capital we represent, or "hold," on behalf of privileged white males. Sexual violence is a staple of patriarchal relations, whereby males wield whatever privilege they have (or wish to appear to have) over others, especially women and children but also other men. Privileged males wield their sexual power by rape, harassment, seduction, wealth, physical force and brutality, and also by the awe, excitement, and fear generated through patriarchy's cross-cultural panorama of art, music, sports, profession, business, entertainment, and religion.

This is the social context in which women of all colors and cultures have learned to fear sexual violence. We do not have to have been raped or battered by a man to know in our body-selves the fear of being followed by a stranger or watched too closely by a voyeur, or of being badgered for sexual favors by a boss or passed over for tenure because we're too feminist, too strong, too much. Women of all colors, classes, and cultures know this fear and, if we're wise, pay attention to it as we move along a day at a

time. It teaches us about our world: about the misogyny and sexist alienation that are structured into our
lives as women in a man's world. (Parenthetically, I
will say here that it's a very *Christian* world I'm
speaking of, the one I know best, but I'm aware that
the *strongest fundamentalist current in all patriarchal
religion, East and West, is formed by merging
streams of misogyny, somatophobia (fear of body)
and erotophobia (fear of the erotic).* Thus, fundamentalist Christians, Jews, and Muslims hold in common
their fear of women, body, and sex.)

So how, in this context, can lesbians expect
possibly to love *our* own bodies or other women's
bodies, or to pleasure ourselves and one another
sexually without fear or apology, delighting with our
sisters in sex for sex's sake? I think we can expect
to be able to delight in our bodies/ourselves/our sex
only insofar as we actively are challenging sexual
abuse *at its root.*

Let me simply list here four patriarchal roots of
sexual violence and abuse:

1) disconnection of sexual yearning from our
experience of the sacred; we experience God
as over/against our sexual appetites;

2) desire for control of our body selves and
those of others; little psychospiritual permis-
sion for imagination, letting go, losing control;

3) experiencing ourselves essentially as isolated, alone, on our own;

4) Justice as benign control, not mutuality and
not non-violent.

I suggest that we lesbians, and gay men as well, face
four simultaneous *theological* tasks if we seriously
are committed to embodying a challenge to these

roots of patriarchy in which sexual violence is promoted and secured. If we omit any one of these tasks, I submit that we cannot satisfactorily respond to the others:

1) *We need to help each other realize that our desire for intimacy, connection, and touch—whether explicitly sexual touching or a more diffuse sensual yearning—is erotic. It is good. And it is sacred.* I have thought about Kathleen Sand's thoughtful critique of Rita Nakashima Brock's and my having sacralized and, in different ways, idealized the erotic.[5] But is the process of valuing not intrinsically a process of sacralizing? We don't have to be theists, certainly not monotheists, to stake high moral claim on our creaturely yearning for intimacy, connection, and touch, and to believe—to assume or imagine—that such desire and such connection "has power" and that this power is basically good—that is, it is creative, and liberating, for everyone. Only insofar as [this sacred power] is "twisted or distorted by patriarchal ideology and lived experience," contends Canadian ethicist Kathryn Pauly Morgan, does it cease being good, for us and for others.[6] Hoagland writes, "I want to suggest that *desire* is neither a matter of being in or out of control, nor need it be a matter of being "safe" or "in danger." Desire is a matter of connection. It is our lesbian desire which moves us to connect one another."[7] We can perhaps encourage each other to *feel* the desire, to *experience* the yearning, to *reach* to connect, without shame and without coercion.

2) *We need to help each other loose our capacities for imagination.* Canadian ethicist Martha Saunders suggests that it is "not simply that we lack imagination, but that we fear the consequences of living our lives to our fullest capacities."[8] Living life to our fullest capacity is, for Dorothee Sölle, to live a life of *phantasie* in which we literally play the future into

being. We generate the conditions for our erotic yearnings to be met. We understand our capacity to god—and we know it is not an autonomous attribute, an individual virtue, a coercive or dishonest overture, but rather a movement, however small, in relational mutuality. Speaking sexually, this is the context in which "erotica" (and Joann Loulan comes at once to mind) can be so helpful to us women, and so sexually freeing: Pictures, possibilities, smells, sounds, tastes, toys, and images to stir, spark and tease our desires to touch and connect, to know and be known, in deep, dark, and mysterious caverns of pleasure and pain, yearning and memory.

3) *We need to build strong expansive communities.* (Notice I use the plural—for most of us move in many directions at once with overlapping circles of colleagues, friends, family, lovers, and others with whom we may draw strength). None of us lesbians can afford much longer, I believe, to allow our needs to be with friends, in community, to take a backseat to pressing obligations. I have come to believe that many of us are *afraid* of community—that is, of participating fully in mutually-empowering circles of friends. Could it be that, in such community, we come face to face with ourselves—our erotically-empowered and empowering *body* selves? Could it be that it has begun to feel "safer" to be simply alone with a lover, or at work, or on the road or on the run or otherwise too busy to sit with one another intimately and yearn for connection and touch? Hoagland says we don't know much about really being with one another as sisters and friends. We don't "attend"9 each other very well most of the time. We go to therapy or become therapists. We turn to religion or become priests, pastors, rabbis, teachers. But do we really know one another, love one another, know how mutually to hold each other's pain, dreams, fears, possibilities, courage?

4) *We need to assume that we will always be struggling for justice in its many forms as mutually empowering connection.* If we are seriously interested in toppling or transforming patriarchal power structures, we need to assume that we will be anti-racist people, we will be anti-sexist and anti-heterosexist people, and our primary interest in capitalism will not be to generate capital for ourselves and "our own" but rather to use whatever resources we have or make toward the transformation of our society—economically, racially, sexually, and otherwise—into a more *non-violent* time and space in history. *Phantasie* indeed! Our primary moral agency—our capacity to do what is more or less right in any given situation—is to help create the yearning and conditions for non-violent, non-abusive life together.

Now, this is a full theological practicum for lesbians and gay men: to learn to feel and honor our erotic desire for intimacy, connection and touching as sacred; to cultivate our *phantasie*, our imagination and intuition, as basic to our lives, love, and work; to build communities, circles of friends, sisters and brothers, with whom we are mutually attentive; and to participate in the ongoing struggles for justice that do not end but rather change with us throughout, and beyond, our lives as individuals and communities.

3. What Lesbians and Gay Men Can Learn from One Another

I believe that gay men can learn from lesbians that love-making is justice-making. The prophetic Presbyterian task force report on sexuality that was defeated overwhelmingly at last summer's General Assembly calls "justice-love"[10] the highest moral good, that which we are here on this earth to help create. Because lesbians not only are marginalized as *homosexual* in a heterosexist and homophobic social order but also are on the bottom of the margins as *women* in a sexist world that is androcentric and misogynist, we lesbians must hold our brothers—gay men and other men—responsible for active participation in the struggle for women's well-being, for gender as well as sexual justice. Over the last two decades, white *feminist* women—lesbians and other women—have begun, through the grace and insistence of our sisters of color, to make connection among the many structures of oppression that divide and wound us, some of us more than others: racism, classism, as well as sexism, heterosexism, and other sources of injustice.

Most gay men, especially white gay men, have much to learn about how these structures of injustice serve to enable white privileged men (including lots of *closeted* gay men and some few *openly* gay men) to secure their privilege—i.e., their economic, gender, and racial power-*over* the rest of us, including lesbians. Not to make these connections is to collude in the maintenance of the conditions that foster sexual violence against women and children, against lesbians, and against gay men. It is difficult for lesbians to interpret gay male "camp" as anything but offensive when it is being played out by men who are either ignorant of, or indifferent to, the ravages of sexism. The "religious divergence" Mary Hunt has addressed today is partially a consequence of the privileged refusal of significant numbers of gay men in religious institutions to take their own gender privilege seriously or to join their lesbian feminist sisters in the movements for gender, racial, and economic justice as well as for "gay rights." More than a few lesbians *have* been alongside our gay brothers in the wrenching, physical, political, emotional, and spiritual struggle against AIDS. How many gay men have been on the front lines with their sisters in the tiresome battle for reproductive freedom? It is not a matter of owing each other favors, or of taking turns. It is a matter of solidarity, of embodying connections.

Only insofar as this is happening can gay men and lesbians even imagine creating communities of colleagues and comrades that would include each other and be mutually empowering for both lesbians and gay men; communities in which, together, gay men and lesbians could perhaps begin to explore together many dimensions of erotic desire and imagination that probably none of us dares to dream at this time. Who knows what we might discover sexually about ourselves and one another, across gender and sexuality lines, in the context of community in which men seriously were interested in justice for women and in bringing patriarchal relations, religion, and culture to an end?

What, in the meantime, this side of that utopia, can lesbians learn from gay men? Just as lesbians can teach gay men that love—erotic power, sacred power—is *justice*, gay men can help lesbians learn to imagine that this same love—this same justice, this same sacred power—is *pleasure*. Not that it *always* feels good, though often it does, but rather that even through pain, trauma, and loss—the suffering brought on by AIDS and by sexual abuse, by heterosexism and racism, by sexism and economic exploitation—even through this immense pain, erotic power can open us to pleasure. Gay men can teach lesbians, I suspect, that *despite* violence and tragedy, abuse and even death, our sacred power moves us toward connection—*"coinherence,"* religiously speaking—through which we learn to experience ourselves as interwoven or, in a language of male sexuality, as inter-penetrated: I in you, you in me. *Pro-feminist* gay males can teach us more, I think, than most lesbians (especially *religious* lesbians) know about how playing sexually with power is *not* necessarily to collude with patriarchal principles of domination and control. It can be a way of embodying some profoundly sacred tensions between our human experiences of controlling and releasing, holding on and letting go, living and dying, our experiences of clarity and mystery, of the known and the unknown, of old and new, of friend and stranger. Pulled back and forth, inside and out, within us and between us, we are in one moment wired and wanting, in the next at peace and filled. This is life, some would say, in god. It is also good sex. I think that many gay men, because they are men in patriarchy, have had an opportunity not to deny or fear their bodies the way we women have learned to experience ours. I think that, for this reason, many gay men often *know* more fully, more deeply, and more ecstatically in relating to one another the "godness" of their erotic power (though they often fail to see its distortions, for example, through sexism and racism into violence). I believe we lesbians have much to learn about our own sexual possibilities, and about the sacred, through friendship with gay men whose lives and values we trust. And while gay men can, with our help, become more fully involved in the struggle for justice as our allies, we lesbians can, perhaps, with the solidarity of our gay brothers, begin to let go of being sexually "correct," quit being good girls, and find out for ourselves, first hand, why patriarchy has repressed us sexually: Once freed, I suspect, we become ever more dangerous women, committed passionately and irrepressibly to both justice and pleasure, unwilling to settle for less.

---

* I want to thank several people especially for having helped me move toward the ideas developed in this paper: Bonnie Engelhardt, Mary Glasspool, Peggy Hanley-Hackenbruck, Bev Harrison, and Myke Johnson.

1 See J.C. Brown and C. Bohn, eds., *Christianity, Patriarchy, and Abuse* (New York, NY: The Pilgrim Press, 1989).

2 Feminists in the U.S. who, to my reading, have contributed in major ways to the shaping of fear-based sexual ethics, include Andrea Dworkin, Catherine MacKinnon, and much of the Women Against Pornography effort of the 1970's and 1980's; Kathleen Barry, Mary Daly, Janice Raymond, and the "sexual correctness" posture of lesbians against S/M in the 1980's; and, more recently, feminist women, and many men as well, in the churches and other religious institutions, and in psychotherapeutic practice, who are attempting to curb sexual misconduct by imposing absolutist rules that prohibit all sexual contact under all circumstances between helping professionals and those who seek help. The problem is three-fold: 1) It reinforces the *power-over* model of professional work and, in so doing, systemically holds patriarchal power in place; 2) It reinforces a *fear* of our bodies, touching, and sex rather than helping empower us to *risk learning how to act responsibly as embodied sexual beings*; and 3) Because it serves primarily to repress rather than to generate serious ethical discourse and responsibility, *it won't work.* Sexual abuse will not be curbed, except perhaps temporarily.

3 Sarah Lucia Hoagland, *Lesbian Ethics: Toward a New Value* (Palo Alto, CA: Institute of Lesbian Studies, 1988), p. 11.

4 Ibid., p. 212.

5 Kathleen M. Sands, "Uses of the Thea(o)logian: Sex and Theodicy in Religious Feminism,"*Journal of Feminist Studies in Religion* 8.1 ((Spring 1992): 7-33.

6 Kathryn Pauly Morgan, "Women and Moral Madness," *Canadian Journal of Philosophy* Supplementary volume 13 (1988): 201.

7 Hoagland, p. 169.

8 Martha J. Saunders, "Sexuality, Justice, and Feminist Ethics," *Resources for Feminist Research* 19.3 & 4 (Sept./Dec. 1990): 37.

9 See Hoagland.

10 See *Presbyterians and Human Sexuality: Response to the Report of the Special Committee on Human Sexuality,*

Including a "Minority Report," (Louisville, KY: Office of the General Assembly, Presbyterian Church [U.S.A.], 1991).

II. Mary E. Hunt:

Opposites Do Not Always Attract:
How and Why Lesbian Women and
Gay Men Diverge Religiously

1. Introduction

The election of a President who favors certain rights
for lesbian/gay/bi-sexual people is a welcome change.
I am not overly optimistic about the impact of an
executive order to recognize the make-up of the
military, and I would prefer an executive order to encourage lesbian/gay/bisexual people on every school
board in the country. However, I am emboldened by
this election to look carefully at the differences between and among lesbian/gay/bisexual people in religion in order to accomplish the historical project of
inclusion.

I highlight differences with a certain caution,
knowing that such efforts can be perceived by those
who seek to divide and conquer as fuel for their fires.
That is not my purpose. To the contrary, my intention
is to name what many have felt, yet been hesitant to
voice for the well-grounded fear that small gains
would evaporate, that fragile alliances would be torn
apart. These are still real possibilities, with the
Religious Right gearing up already for 1996 after
having run "stealth candidates" in 1992 and
planning to introduce Colorado-style legislation in
Oregon and other states to roll back lesbian/gay civil
rights.

More than ever, those of us who engage in the
praxis of justice-making need a clear sense of who
we are in order to assure our collective survival. I
make no apology for using scholarly apparatus and

academic settings to advance such an agenda; I urge
others to be equally responsible.

2. State of the Problem

Lesbian women and gay men are treated as a unit in
churches, synagogues and other religious groups that
look at issues related to homosexuality, such as ordination or same-sex unions. I am less persuaded that
opposites always attract, that this combination is always in our best interests, especially in women's best
interests. I am increasingly convinced that this is an
"arranged marriage" between same-sex loving
women and men which may profit from mediation
unto divorce in the best interests of the children. This
is necessary so that we can emerge as friends and
colleagues on an equal footing, rather than marriage
partners who, like many heterosexually married
couples, struggle with the structural inequalities of
patriarchy which still usually render women as junior
partners and give men an inflated sense of themselves.

In this essay I do not separate out differences by
age, race or location, though such differences exist as
the emerging lesbian womanist work shows. Rather,
for purposes of making the most general argument, I
seek to sketch the contours of the problem so that
others can, using the hint, explain and change the
dynamic at play.

As the movement for lesbian/gay ecclesial rights
has matured, most mainline Christian denominations
have found themselves with a lesbian/gay caucus or
organization for spiritual and social support; increasingly those groups include bi-sexual and transgender
people as well. Most groups have a newsletter and
lobby efforts to hasten their members' full inclusion
into the body of the denomination.

Results have been mixed, and criteria for success vary from painful defeats in the Presbyterian Church (U.S.A.) to the highly successful strategy of starting a new denomination, the Metropolitan Community Church. Still, that the MCC cannot join nor even observe the National Council of Churches signals that there is still plenty of "holy homo-hatred" to go around.

There are now interdenominational efforts including *Open Hands* and *Second Stone* magazines, and national coalitions of the various groups. Christian Lesbians Out Together (CLOUT) is an active newcomer. Ecumenical ministries exist such as Spectrum under the able leadership of the Rev. Jane Adams Spahr, who was recently rejected for a pastorate to which she was called in a remarkable show of Presbyterians acting so like Catholic hierarchs as to pose the possibility of a schism within that communion.

At a time when mainline churches find themselves on the wane and in difficult economic times, lesbian/gay/bisexual people have proved ourselves to be good for business. For example, the fastest growing United Church of Christ congregation in the United States is Spirit of the Lakes in Minneapolis/St. Paul, a predominantly lesbian/gay/bisexual community. Liberal denominations and "open and affirming" churches eventually realize that lesbian/gay/bisexual people as an economic cohort give generously, just as politicians have discovered that we vote "early and often." This is not a trivial component of what small increase in openness can be noted in some churches.

I am part of and supportive of many of these efforts. However, it is my contention that in patriarchal religions, in this case Christianity, such efforts have been flawed and progress retarded by the conceptual errors of using what I call "lumpen lesbian" and "generic gay" categories. Specifically, for purposes of patriarchal religions, women, including lesbians, have always been collapsed into men's categories in order to count, and male experience, including gay male experience, has always defined the norm.

While this kind of insight is now axiomatic after twenty years of feminist/womanist/mujerista work in religion, it is an important recognition for historians and activists alike as lesbian/gay church history unfolds. Historians need to take the differences seriously in order to correct the record, to show, for example, that lesbian women were doing lots of other things spiritual at the same time that patriarchal churches were being integrated. For example, the writings of Pat Parker, May Sarton, Audre Lorde and Adrienne Rich, all open and affirming lesbian women and none of them religious professionals, have nourished many people spiritually.

Activists need to recognize the real differences in experiences, trajectories and spiritual desires on the part of women and men so that we may hear and support one another on our own terms. We may not always like what we hear, but at the moment we are still kept from the full conversation. Reasons are clear: on the one hand, a laudable effort to present a united front for survival and solidarity; and on the other hand, and this is my concern, at the expense of possible new directions which I believe should emerge for our common, albeit at times separate, growth.

Further, I note that as a result of this situation, a problem we have prudently, charitably and now long enough hidden, the trajectory for lesbian/gay/bisexual people in religion is more rather than less gender-bound, with many lesbian women increasingly moving away from mainline Christianity and many gay men finding increasing comfort there. I do not wish to claim here more than I can prove; data are limited. But if the literature and the anecdotal and analytic evidence are taken together, there is at least a serious conversation to be had.

For this preliminary study I confine myself to so-called mainline Christianity although I suspect that the same dynamic is operative in Judaism and other religious traditions as well. I tend to look most closely at Catholic data both because I know it best and because in Catholicism male/female, clergy/lay, gay/straight lines are tightly and clearly drawn, a dubious advantage, but helpful nonetheless for showing the contours of misogyny and homo-hatred that are present, if less obvious, in other denominations.

3. *Erroneous Assumptions and Why They Work*

The erroneous lumping of lesbian women and gay men, and the resultant generic "gay" as a category, is a mistake of some duration. I will leave it to the Ann Matters and John Boswells to say just how long and where. But taking the past two decades when homo-activism has been most vigorous in the churches, there is an obvious and troubling trend. Note that this is a period roughly parallel to the development of feminist, now also womanist and mujerista, theology which was supposed to be an antidote to male hegemony.

Interestingly, the prevalence of "lumpen lesbian" and "generic gay" categories persists through what I see as three distinct moments in the rapid and creative development of lesbian/gay, later including bi-sexual thought: homosexual stage, lesbian/gay stage (usually gay/lesbian but I'm trying to break the pattern), and now the queer stage. Note that the dates I am suggesting are preliminary, and there is undoubtedly overlapping of the three periods; my point is simply to name and outline three distinct periods and claim that the dynamic to which I am pointing has not changed significantly.

4. *Homosexual Stage (1972-1982)*

Early contemporary efforts to deal with Christianity and same-sex love emerged under the rubric John McNeill coined in his pioneering work *The Church and the Homosexual* (1976).[1] Homosexuality is seen as a problem for churches, with celibacy the churches' solution. Not only do church documents reflect the standard "the homosexual he," but lesbian women as such simply do not appear on our own terms. This is understandable, even expected for such pioneering efforts which were crafted in response to prevailing clinical notions, much of it researched if not published before the American Psychological and American Psychiatric Associations declassified homosexuality as mental illness. That the early literature did not distinguish female from male experience is not shocking.

However, several factors other than the obvious sexism make it puzzling. Lesbian writers, notably Sally Gearhart, who wrote the first essay on the topic, "The Lesbian and God the Father or All the Church Needs is a Good Lay—On Its Side," were very explicit about their sexual politics and their sexuality.[2] A non-ordained professor of speech does not attract media attention like an ordained Jesuit priest; she does not exist ecclesially in the same way. Hence such writing simply did not find its way into the predominantly male sources which have become the sacred texts of the church-based movement.

Women writers as well as men in this early stage participated in the obscuring of women's experiences and the "homosexual equals male equals all" approach. With all due respect, Letha Scanzoni and Virginia Ramey Mollenkott in their popular book *Is the Homosexual My Neighbor?* (1978) make no substantive distinctions between women and men in their analysis.[3] Rather, the effort, laudable as it is, resulted in equal opportunity liberation in an unequal world and church.

Denominational groups like Dignity and Integrity which began during this period are theo-political mirrors of this dynamic. With some notable exceptions, male leadership was common, male ministers normative. Social and spiritual life in these groups was geared to what churchmen needed, namely a place to worship "just like home" except that the denomination's teachings were tinkered with on the matter of homosexual love, and a clubby environment to fulfill what many a mother told her marriage-age daughter: "Meet a nice boy in church."

It is important to point out that during this period (and to this day in some denominations like Roman Catholicism) female ministers were in short supply. Likewise, during this period lesbian women had many other options for spirituality from the then nascent women-church movement to women's spirit groups and wicca, all of which lessened our dependence on patriarchal churches but did not have an appreciable impact on how the "homosexual question" was dealt with within churches.

Nonetheless, those women who participated in the church-based organizations did so on male terms as homosexuals, both in terms of having their sexuality subsumed although their sexual forays were probably a fraction of what some men's were (though in many cases the male's were grossly exaggerated), and their proximity to church power, namely, access to church leaders, mostly male, was nil compared with reports from some gay men, who, to hear tell, were in some instances hand in glove, as it were.

These several differences, while passed over to build a movement, resulted in documents, organizations and efforts at ecclesial change which, while nominally for women and men, were based on male models of ministry and priesthood, sexuality and structures of power, especially economic.

5. *Lesbian/Gay/Bisexual Stage (1982-1992)*

This dynamic changed slightly in the second period, what I call the lesbian/gay/bisexual stage. No longer could one argue that lesbian experience was not accessible. The explicitly lesbian feminist perspectives articulated in books and collections of essays by Carter Heyward, Janice Raymond, Barbara Zanotti, Cherrie Moraga and Gloria Anzaldua, Rosemary Curb and Nancy Manahan, Mary Daly, Evelyn Torton Beck, Virginia Ramey Mollenkott, Mary E. Hunt and many others provided information aplenty for the "feministization" of the churches and synagogues, as well as the adoption of same-sex love as healthy, good, natural and holy from a lesbian perspective.[4]

Groups like the Conference for Catholic Lesbians, and later CLOUT, formed to give voice to women when the existing groups retained patriarchal styles, practices and commitments longer than women's patience would bear. Despite the spate of literature and the insistence on substantive changes, not simply cosmetic ones by women, changes in structure not simply changes in form (concretely, new ways to be church, not simply new people to be church), the contours of church-related issues for most religious lobby groups remained relatively static.

The ordination question is a good example. In the Presbyterian, Episcopal and Methodist Churches the issue is still framed to ordain or not to ordain "self-affirming, practicing" lesbian and gay people.

There is no real discussion of ordination in itself. In the Catholic case it is even more pernicious since no women, lesbian or heterosexual, are ordained.

There has been a deafening silence from gay male priests on this question, due of course to their (correct) perception that their own ministries are in danger. But given their majority status (data is scarce but this is commonly assumed since the clerical exodus after Vatican II was predominantly heterosexual), and given the overwhelming range of Catholic feminist theology, it is all the more remarkable that efforts at change are, finally, so timid.

Substantive feminist concerns about the connection between orders and jurisdiction, the dubious assumption of hierarchy, and the continuation of clericalism with openly gay clerics instead of closeted ones are simply ignored. It is commonplace to say that people who have been barred must seek entrance on the owners' terms, hence the focus on simply ordaining lesbian and gay people and assuming that change will come later. But curiously, in the case of the churches, because gay male experience coincides with straight male experience far more than it does with feminist experience whether lesbian, heterosexual or bisexual, it is what holds sway even when the ordinands are women.

For example, when the Rev. Elizabeth Carl was ordained as an openly lesbian priest in the Episcopal Church there was little to distinguish her ordination from the usual administration of the sacrament, although one should not pass over Elizabeth's own powerful presence and style. Similarly, with the Rev. Jane Adams Spahr, the most important aspect of her case is lost when only the issue of lesbian/gay ordination is put forward. I would guess that it is her feminist style as much as her lesbianism that is being rejected. But this is passed over at our peril, I believe, as if muddying the waters with issues other than sexual orientation is hazardous to progress. To the contrary, it is precisely what is at play when we look critically at what many lesbian women, as well as many straight and bi-sexual women, not to mention some men, are saying about ecclesial change. That many of us have voted with our feet is due as much to these broader issues as to the exclusion of lesbian/gay people.

The strongest parallels exist to the integration of the military. Women in disproportionately large numbers have been drummed out of the Marine Corps (estimates are that 6 women are dismissed for every man even though gay males probably outnumber lesbian women by the tens of thousands). Likewise, women have been disproportionately disenfranchised by church policies. Yet women have provided "coming out" leadership from The Rev. Joan Clark,[5] to the ordination cases I mentioned, as well as in a celebrated Lutheran case when a lesbian couple was ordained.

Important as it is, none of this reflects the deeper issues that are central to feminist work: questions about power structures, especially racism and class divisions, fundamental matters like clergy/lay difference, intercommunion which is virtually a non-issue among lesbian feminists, eclectic spirituality including Goddess, wiccan and New Age elements woven unapologetically into Christian practice, and the less tangible matters such as worship style—circles rather than rows, dialogues rather than sermons—and feminist styles of pastoral counselling. Many lesbian/gay/bisexual organizations have begun to deal with these issues and progress is discernable. But in the lesbian/gay stage the very definition of the problems is still more generic gay than not.

No one, including myself, likes to bring attention to the fact that most of the church-related lesbian/gay/bisexual groups are far from being gender-balanced; "where have all the women gone?" is an oft-sung hymn. Just this week when the Catholic groups Dignity and New Ways Ministry delivered thousands of petitions demanding lesbian/gay civil rights to the bishops, the participants were mostly male with a solidarity smattering of women-church, mostly heterosexual women who were attending the meeting to lobby the same bishops on reproductive rights, about which the men's groups still have scruples.

This points out the primary problem, namely, that even as we approach the end of the second decade there is still deep lack of mutual understanding, especially with regard to issues like abortion and pay equity which are, wrongly, percieved to be women's issues, and anti-racism work which has become central to feminist work. It is not simply that these issues in and of themselves make a major difference in terms of priorities, but taken together with issues related to sexual orientation they reconfigure the whole agenda. For example, as a lesbian feminist I am equally troubled by the Catholic Church's position on abortion as on homosexuality; making a church safe for "out" gay priests, as opposed to closeted ones does not mean that episcopal lobby efforts to defeat legal abortion will cease. I do not need to choose between the two issues, but I expect cooperation on both. As a white woman I am equally as troubled by right-wing racism as by right-wing homophobia. I do not divide my efforts by working on both, but double them for our collective survival.

AIDS has played a central role in redirecting religious lesbian/gay efforts toward the concrete needs—physical, spiritual and legislative—of our whole community and in reasserting the urgency of inclusion. This is as it should be. But it means that once more, and tragically, the gay male agenda predominates. Of course the web of care has been extended to women and children, and non-gay men who are HIV+, but the flavor and focus of the efforts is decidedly male as one would expect.

This is a delicate matter as I am certain that gay men would have long ago traded any privilege they might have to spare even one death from AIDS. But the fact remains that the pandemic has added to the male-centeredness of the movement as evidenced by the kinds of healing services, prayer books, wakes, funerals and support groups that have emerged as a much-needed response. I never cease to be moved by the power of the ministry, but I am increasingly bothered by the language, imagery, music, format and leadership, which, with notable exceptions, seem unchanged, indeed almost unaffected by the feminist work of the past few decades. By contrast, the ministry, meaning and community surrounding women dealing with breast and ovarian cancer show clear signs of being shaped by lesbian feminist spirituality. The play "CancerBodies" by Victoria Rue is an early example of this growing phenomenon.

The good news is that the same male money, access to media, business, the arts, even to church, has been directed to the gargantuan, and still minuscule, efforts to eradicate the disease and the homo-hatred it has inspired and permitted. However, as we move into the queer stage, I am hopeful that we can avoid repeating the mistake of "lumpen lesbian" and "generic gay," and in so doing move to a qualitatively new approach to religion. Otherwise, I suggest that we let our roads diverge according to gender and not pretend otherwise.

6. *Queer Stage (1992-??)*

The so-called queer stage is where we find ourselves today. This is due to the important if debated influence of Act-Up and its cousins, of mostly younger lesbian/gay/bisexual people who see no reason, and I as a middle-aged cheer leader with them, to tolerate the constraints of gender roles, compulsory monogamy and desexualized politics. It is exciting to think that whole new categories can emerge for discussion since the boredom that results from explaining the same tired truths about how we are not all promiscuous pedophiles after all is part of a strategy to wear us down.

However, to an alarming degree the same pattern is repeating itself: queer, like homosexual and gay before it, has been a generic as well as particular word for males, as in "lezzies and queers." Note we are not at the lesbian stage of things with "lesbian" becoming generic for a change, signalling a serious grappling with women's experiences. Rather, in the first queer theological book, *Jesus Acted Up: A Gay and Lesbian Theological Manifesto*[6] by Robert E. Goss, there is clear acknowledgement of the problem of false inclusion, even disagreement with my suggestion that we not make claims for one another, women and men, at least not now. But what follows is an analysis which uses some of the tools of feminist theology but misses both the trends away from Christian theology and toward far broader religious categories. I was reminded of Mary Daly's response to Leonard Swidler's article "Jesus was a Feminist" to which she put the question, "So what?" I asked myself, "*Jesus Acted Up.* So what?" If queer theology is "in your face" Christianity, does it really reflect lesbian feminist experiences? If not, fine, but let's be frank and not repeat the unhelpful pattern of false inclusion.

The churches are still debating homosexuality; many progressive people have gotten as far as lesbian/gay consciousness. But the queer stage adds three major novelties to the mix which I think point a way beyond the current stasis. Let me conclude with these as suggestive of a constructive way to acknowledge the divergence I have outlined, and at the same time to use it creatively.

1. Queer includes more than lesbian women and gay men. It is an umbrella term, how broad remains to be seen, to include bi-sexual people as a real constituency, not as a transitional category. It includes drag queens, cross dressers and transvestites, trans

sexuals and other so-called sexual minorities. In the face of such diversity, gender differences shrink somewhat. In short, it has the potential to collapse even more people into a male mold, or to turn the mold inside out by encouraging as much diversity on its own terms as possible. That is a formidable task for already beleaguered lesbian and gay clergy, for example, who must now make room, and take hostility, for and sometimes from the more marginal members of our extended community. Here women who have less to lose will lead the way, but I urge this on gay men lest we simply make a little bit of room for ourselves and end up hopelessly coopted.

2. Queer also derives from a highly nuanced understanding of sexuality, including sexual orientations (shifts over time in one person, changing historical patterns within cultures, etc.) and practices for which theologians and ethicists are only starting to look for, much less find, a vocabulary. Sado-masochism as feminist activity is one with which I, if you will pardon the expression, wrestle, not sure how to hold the two notions together, but willing, indeed obliged, to participate in the discussion with an open mind and ready ethical resources.

These matters require far more than simply recasting the circle or recycling Jesus as queer. They invite engagement with a range of religious traditions and ways of shaping meaning and value. They require familiarity with the deconstructed universe of postmodernism from which some of the claims proceed, and they invite participation in a world of practices and commitments which remain unexplored. They require a firm grappling with the different experiences that African American lesbian women like Renee Hill and Sandra Robinson bring to the mix.

At the very least, queer consciousness is a clean break from the tyranny of twosomes and the need to defend something as essential about oneself as one's sexuality. However, whether queer consciousness is more than that, indeed whether it is a step toward greater inclusivity or just greater diversity for those who can afford it, is what remains to be seen. If religious organizations are bogged down with false assumptions when there is only a two-way gender difference, I am not optimistic about their being able to deal with the multidimensional discussions which are in the offing.

3. Queer consciousness and the theo-ethical work that emerges from it can be qualitatively different if those who have grounded the discussion in homosexual experience and taken it to the lesbian/gay stage will correct past errors and move along honestly even if it means separate paths for a while. Not all queers are created equal: queer women, queer members of oppressed racial-ethnic groups, and those queers whose behaviors and beings do not conform to the slightly altered at the altar generic male norm are fast approaching a critical mass.

Many who were born as queer Christians have been so scandalized by the anti-queer churches that we have left our denominations and are developing new ways to be religious. Likewise, many queers who are deeply involved in churches can embrace their queerness and in so doing shift the strategies from incremental inroads to substantive structural changes. Still other queers who have never been involved with churches, or who are involved with other religious traditions, bring still more insights to the reconstruction of Christianity.

7. Conclusion

The problems I have named and clarified are success problems. They result from the efforts of homosexual, lesbian/gay/bisexual and now queer people, our supporters and colleagues, to transform patriarchal, homo-hating churches and ideologies into embracing communities and inclusive theologies. If the next step is to admit our differences as women and men in order to sort out our strengths, the one after that is to find our commonalities to bolster our respective weaknesses. The historic American Academy of Religion session joining Lesbian Feminist Issues and Gay Men's Issues in Religion Groups for the first time was a good and trustworthy place to begin the public professional conversation. The challenge is to keep it going, to include more people and to manage the whole thing without falling prey to those who would spin it to seem as if we hate one another.

1 John McNeill, *The Church and the Homosexual* (Kansas City, MO: Sheed, Andrews and McMeel, 1976).

2 Sally Miller Gearhart, "The Lesbian and God-the-Father or all the Church Needs is a Good Lay--on its Side," in *Genesis III* [Newsletter of the tri-faith Philadelphia Task Force on Women in Religion], supplement to May-June 1973 issue, 1973.

3 Virginia Ramey Mollenkott and Letha Scanzoni, *Is the Homosexual my Neighbor?* (New York: Harper and Row, 1978).

4 A lesbian issues in religion bibliography would include, though not be limited to: Carter Heyward, *Speaking of Christ* (New York: The Pilgrim Press, 1989); Janice Raymond, *A Passion for Friends* (Boston: Beacon Press, 1985); Barbara Zanotti, ed., *A Faith of One's Own* (Trumansburg, NY: The Crossing Press, 1986); Cherrie Moraga and Gloria Anzaldua, eds., *This Bridge Called my Back* (Watertown, MA: Persephone Press, 1981); Rosemary Curb and Nancy Manahan, eds., *Lesbian Nuns: Breaking Silence* (Tallahassee, FL: Naiad Press, 1985); Mary Daly, *Pure Lust* (Boston: Beacon Press, 1984); Evelyn Torton Beck, ed., *Nice Jewish Girls* (Trumansburg, NY: The Crossing Press, 1982); Virginia Ramey Mollenkott, *Sensuous Spirituality* (NY: Crossroad, 1992); Mary E. Hunt, *Fierce Tenderness: A Feminist Theology of Friendship* (NY: Crossroad, 1991).

5 Joan L. Clark, "Coming Out: The Process and its Price," *Christianity and Crisis* 39.10 (1979): 149-153.

6 Robert E. Goss, *Jesus Acted Up: A Gay and Lesbian Theological Manifesto* (San Francisco, CA: HarperCollins, 1993).

III. Michael L. Stemmeler:

"Family" in the Gay Nineties: The Explosion of a Concept

1. Introduction

So Murphy Brown had a baby. The child, as far as I know—and I am not an authority on TV-sitcoms—is still without name,[1] nevertheless it seems to be fully integrated into all aspects of Murphy Brown's life: from the home to the office to the luncheon place. Murphy Brown is very concerned about the welfare of her baby. So is almost everybody else in her office. Seems like a pretty decent family. Or is it? What then makes a family? And if we can ever figure out what makes a family, will we be able to establish what "family values" are, or better, what they should be.

For the sake of inclusiveness let me quote freely from what Barbara Bush said in her address to the 1992 Republican Convention in Houston. Remember, both her talk and ex-vice-presidential life-mate Marilyn Quale's speech were specifically advertised as addresses to the American public on so-called "family values." In a nutshell, Barbara Bush said that "family values"—and I do not quote *verbatim*—are everything you label as "family values." For the ex-presidential household that means in Barbara Bush's own words: "We just hug a lot and support each other." For 'ole times' sake and to placate a particular political constistency a little prayer was also thrown into the equation. Barbara Bush's definition sounds like what every "decent" American would probably have said about family and family values, religion and all. The majority of the American people seem to think right along the lines of the billboard advertisement which reads: "A family that prays together stays together."

In a National Public Radio report in the fall of 1992 during the heat of the election campaign, a representative from the American Family Institute, an ideologically reactionary and religiously fanatic think-tank, was asked to define "family values." The definition was fairly simple and was for the most part made up of "hugging, loving, kissing, supporting," and, yes also again, "praying." The definition was then read to a number of people from different walks of life without revealing the source of the definition. You may not be surprised to hear that everyone interviewed about the definition had not the slightest objections to it. Some would emphasize the supporting part more than the praying part. Others talked more about love as a general disposition and less about hugging as specific acts of showing that loving affection. In essence, however, there was great agreement about the accuracy of the definition.

The most striking response came from two lesbian women in Florida, one of whom a lawyer, who had adopted a child and was raising it together with her partner. One of the women responded on the radio: "Yeah, that's what I understand as family values." The question now can be asked: "Does the presence of these values in the relationships in which I, as a gay person, engage, be they vertical or horizontal relationships, create family?" Asked differently: "Is 'family' the appropriate descriptor for loving and supporting relationships in which there is a lot of hugging, kissing, and spiritual understanding?"

These questions have to be asked with all urgency by lesbian, gay, and bisexual people who have throughout history formed relationships that bore the above mentioned characteristics. Yet until this day their relationships have not received official legal and/or public/social recognition. More recently some gay-friendly religious communities have begun to voice cautious words of welcome to lesbian, gay and bisexual people engaged in non-traditional relationships. Gay affirmative religious communities have for a number of years bestowed spiritual recognition to relationships of affection and affinity among lesbians and gays. But it will not be enough merely to ask the questions. Answers will have to be provided by lesbian, gay and bisexual people themselves if they want to forestall attempts to have their relationships first defined and then (negatively) judged by the social, legal, and moral standards of the surrounding heterosexual and heterosexist world.

2. *The Family We Have Come to Loathe*

Most everyone in America is familiar with the Norman Rockwell painting of the family sitting around the Thanksgiving dinner table, with happy Christian faces, getting ready to attack a dead roasted bird. In that picture the familial roles of the participants are easily identifiable. Grandfather stands at the head of the table, carving knife and fork, the weapons of attack, are positioned in front of him, and he can hardly wait until grandmother places the tray on the table so that the dissecting feast can begin. Grandmother, by the way, swings the dead, yet nicely trimmed bird onto the dinner table with the experienced routine of a circus juggler.

Soon the carving utensils will be in grandfather's hands and he will re-enact some of the remnant rituals of his hunting culture ancestors. He will symbolically kill the bird a second time, carve it up, and distribute the pieces of meat according to rank and worthiness among the family members. Grandfather's place in the ritualized action of bird killing, dissecting, and distributing the food assures him the continuation of his dominant role in the family environment. After all, he is the one who will wield the instruments of power and submission.

Grandfather as the head of the household assumes quasi-divine status in the role of decision maker over life and death. Despite the fact that he features such a benign and truly "grandfatherly" face, he may just as well turn into a fierce hunter who will prove his manhood in the act of killing what needs to be sacrificed for the sake of his family, the continued well-being of which is his social responsibility.

By extension we can see this applied to the next-generation fathers who are sitting already around the table. The poor turkey, despite being depicted as the centerpiece of the picture, is the annual victim in the dominant heterosexual male's quest for power and demands for subjection.

The hierarchical and arch-patriarchal structure of the picture is underlined by the behavior of the other attendants at the dinner. Several generations are represented. Women and children are portrayed in almost equal numbers. We do not know the types of legal relationships portrayed in this picture. But we have certain clues: Since the Thanksgiving dinner is portrayed in the picture, and since Thanksgiving is the family holiday *par excellence* in the United States it is safe to assume that the individuals portrayed in the picture are either consanguinal relatives or relatives through legally recognized marital affinity.

Imagine the presence of a gay son in this cherished family picture. He can already see the knife in his own father's hand. He is rightfully scared in the face of such death-dealing power although he masks his fear with a happy smile. He knows that if his secrets, which—given his late pubescent age—are of course all of a sexual nature, become known to his natural law-of-union-for-procreation abiding father all chances for a fulfilling love and sex life will vanish in a stream of blood gushing from his groin right after his father has laid the knife on him and in turkey-proven manner castrated the nature-defying son.

This daring extended interpretation of Norman Rockwell's Thanksgiving family gathering picture is, admittedly, a somewhat unorthodox and graphic description of the mode in which the idea, ideal, and stereotype of family is perpetuated in the American social context. It is an image of family which veils all the problems and inadequacies of the nuclear family.

Granted, the picture portrays members of three generations. However, it also portrays family as nothing else but white, heterosexual, and middle class. But what in the portrayal of family in America, one may ask, is not defined by these characteristics? This does not take into consideration that more than 30% of all households in the United States are headed by single people, many of whom are involved in raising a generation of children for whom the Norman Rockwell portrayal of family is probably more alien than a report of the landing of the Martians on a New Jersey highway in Orson Welles' radio dramatization of H. G. Wells' *War of the Worlds*. And it also does not account for the ethnic and class varieties of families in the United States. The imagined portrayal of one African-American in the picture maketh not racial justice and equality.

Why are lesbians and gays so much more likely to loathe the kinds of families they grew up in and with? Few of us would deny that there were great and unforgettable moments of love, support, and understanding in our biological families. And still, many of us treat them now with scorn and rejection. Why is this so? And why is it that often, once we have ventilated our anger and voiced our rage against the heterosexual institution of marriage and its family companion, have severed all ties to these oppressive arrangements, we stumble head over heels into new more or less exclusive relationships, establish neo-urban households with all the either yuppy or alternatively dynamic trimmings required, and end up building our own lesbian and gay Rockwellian images of family life. The "way we never were"—to use the title of a recent book by Stephanie Coontz—turns out to be the "way we perhaps were all along," only now outside the heterosexually defined relationship of affinity called marriage.

I feel pressed, however, to make a critical remark at this time. Perhaps it is just due to my very subjective perspective, but when I look at the lives of many—granted, not all—of my lesbian friends, I cannot deny observing a certain "rage for relationships." Their craving for a relationship appears to be a mode of behavior which is quite alien to your "average" gay male who either prides his independence or who, once a partnership has been established, may remain less likely to conduct it on a level of monogamous fidelity as I have come to know it among my lesbian sisters.

The family we have come to loathe is for many of us the biological family into which we were born, which we didn't choose, but to which we, perhaps, chose to come out as lesbians or gays at some point during our life. Whomsoever we encountered in this family environment was encountered as somebody with whom we shared close familial ties based on our joint biogenetical heritage. But we always experienced this family member as different due to the hermeneutical problems inherent in relationships between gay and non-gay people, even if there is a shared biogenetical heritage.

In analogy to Paulo Freire's assigning the hermeneutical privilege of having a clear understanding of liberation and freedom to the oppressed person,[2] I propose the assignment of a hermeneutical privilege to the lesbian or gay person who as a natural/biological member of a family knows what "family" *really* is and what kind of relationships ultimately deserve the label "family ties." This, of course, does not mean, that biological and kinship

relationships are *de facto* excluded from our definition of family. They alone, however, will no longer
deserve to be recognized as exclusively family making.

The family we have come to loathe is the biological family which rejects us because we are lesbian or
gay. It is the family which disestablishes the familial
ties with us, not because we are not able to hug and
love, support and sacrifice ourselves for the members
of our biological family. We experience rejection by
our biological families because they reject the
definition of our identity which incorporates our
identity as sexual beings, and perceives this definition
as a mortal threat to the socio-legal and religious
institution family, which defines itself as both a relationship of affinity through heterosexual marital
bonds and as a relationship of consanguinity. Being
who we are does not provide us with a rationale in a
definition of family which is primarily supported by
the jointly existing traditional ideas of *union* and *procreation,* regardless of the facts that both ideas can be
and are present in many lesbian/gay "family" relationships, or—and this may be more of an indict-
ment—that they are conspicuously absent in many
heterosexual family relationships.

The formation of family and familial relationships
is then not dependent on satisfying the criteria established by the heterosexual dominant society, affinity
and consanguinity, but is exclusively dependent upon
an individual's sexual orientation. Viewed from this
perspective it becomes clear that lesbian and gay
people reject the traditional institution family because
they are able to locate and name the hypocrisy with
which it portrays itself in public. Having a homosexual orientation prevents the lesbian or gay person
from having her/his potential for love, sharing, and
support recognized as family making and sustaining
potential. As in many other social environments, so
here are gay people reduced, through acts of separation by the heterosexual dominant majority, to the

sexual orientation dimension of their lives, an important, nevertheless not exclusively defining dimension.

3. Families We Create and Choose

Right on the opening pages of her book *Families We Choose: Lesbian, Gays, Kinship,*[3] Kath Weston quotes openly gay Boston City Councilor David Scondras as saying that he would work toward gaining recognition for an extended concept of family.[4] From here on Weston, an anthropologist from Arizona State University, researches what the concept of family actually is which underlies Scondras' quotation and which needs to be extended in order to accommodate the loving and supporting relationships of lesbians and gays. "Family" needs to be defined *a priori* before practical application to whatever kinds of relationships can take place. The challenges to come up with a definition of family present themselves at the outset in Weston's work:

> What is the relation of a newly emergent discourse to social movements and social change? Are gay families inherently assimilationists, or do they represent a radical departure from more conventional understandings of kinship? Will gay families have any effect on kinship relations and social relations in the United States as a whole?[5]

As both the title of her work and this quotation indicate, there is no doubt in her mind that families exist *for* gays and lesbians and that, in fact, *gay families* exist. What has not been clarified as of now is the mode in which gay/lesbian families exist. After all, the presence of a gay or lesbian family member itself could conceivably make a gay or lesbian family, if viewed from a linguistically essentialist perspective.

Weston realized early on in her research that there is a pluriformity of definitions of family operating in the United States. No standardized, uniform version of kinship exists which could be called "the American family."[6]

> The standardized "American family" is a mythological creature, but also—like its reified subsidiaries ("the" black family, "the" gay family)—an ideologically potent category.[7]

Based on the research results of Jane Collier and Sylvia Yanagisako in their 1987 article, "Toward a Unified Analysis of Gender and Kinship,"[8] she asserts that "families should not be confounded with genealogically defined relationships."[9]

Not only can one realize a pluriformity of family definitions operating in the United States, but through her interviewing research it became clear to Weston that,

> gay families could not be understood apart from the families in which lesbians and gay men had grown up. After looking at the entire universe of relations they considered kin, it became evident that discourse on gay kinship defines gay families vis-à-vis another type of family known as "straight," "biolo-gical," or "blood"—terms that many gay people applied to their families of origin.[10]

From here on Weston's book embarks on a long journey through multiple manifestations of relationships among lesbians and gay men which the people who are involved in such relationship often, though not always, label "family." One of the guiding questions for her investigative analysis of the chosen family is whether the phrase,

> "related by blood or marriage" [will] be allowed to stand as a justification for refusing lovers public accommodations; denying them visiting rights at nursing homes, prisons, and hospitals; disqualifying gay families for family discounts; or withholding the right to pass on a rent-controlled apartment after death?[11]

If there is no standardized version of family in America it may only be logical to analogize Barbara Bush's remarks about family values also to the institution itself from which these values are supposedly developed: "Families are whatever you create and recognize as families." It may well be, as Weston has observed, that gay and lesbian familial relationships are developed in protest and opposition to a dominant hetero understanding of family.

Nevertheless, exactly in the decision to define our own relationships likewise as familial relationships, as families, in opposition to the dominant hetero family structure—variations to a greater or lesser degree granted—in which we all grew up and, more importantly, in which we all were socialized, we agree to an essentially defining function of our relationship by some version of the straight family concept-cluster. We tacitly accept some of the characteristics which define and create the hetero understanding of family: affinity and consanguinity. This elevates the hetero understanding of family in an undue manner by subjecting our honest relationships of affinity on the one and protest against hetero family imperialism on the other hand to standards which are not our standards. It presents us with ideals which we are socially, legally, and religiously, at least so far, prevented from achieving.

The "explosion" of the family concept, now, is brought about by gays and lesbians who see their familial relationships neither exclusively nor comprehensively defined by either of the above mentioned characteristics. Nor does the presence of these characteristics in their relationships in all cases create family. Thereby the familial relationships of gays and lesbians become irreducible to hetero-defined reductionism. The gay family concept achieves significant distinction through the inclusion of lovers and friends, spouses and play-mates, significant others and buddies or girl-friends, yes and even dogs, cats and vegetable gardens into its definitions of family and into gay and lesbian family networks.

I want to clarify, however, that family networks and familial relationships engaged in by lesbians and gays should not be understood as picking the next best apple from the tree if the—hetero understood—best apple, the heterosexually defined institution of family based exclusively on marital affinity and consanguinity, is not available. I disagree with J. Michael Clark's presentation of lesbian and gay family networks as *surrogate* networks.[12] Gay and lesbian family networks are not a surrogate, they are not a substitute occupying the place of the real thing. They are the most appropriate and—although I do not like to use the term excessively—the most *natural* manifestations of family which exist for lesbian and gay people.

I concur with Clark, however, when he says that long term committed gay and lesbian couples and (more extended) family networks pose a radical challenge to hetero-reductionism of gay and lesbian life to obsessive occupation with the physicality of sexual expression. Neither physical-sexual expression geared toward recreation or procreation, nor loving affection and emotionally or economically supportive behavior alone or in combination are sufficient for the creation of a family. However, all these characteristics and more can be observed individually and are often found collectively in relationships among lesbians or gays to which the label "family" becomes attached.[13]

One of the prime tasks for those gays and lesbians in chosen families is to avoid falling into the trap of judgmental exclusivism. It is a well-known defining feature of patriarchal hetero imperialism to ascribe *reality status* to everything only from its own vantage point. Reality status is ascribed gradually with qualitative differences regarding to how close and how well an emerging entity imitates, assimilates, and incorporates the structures of the defining agency.

In the discussion of lesbian and gay families, this mostly means what sexual policy is embraced. If the gay family assimilates the sexual monogamy ideal of hetero-patriarchal sexual morality it will probably fare better with regard to some level of recognition. Value increments are assigned which place the monogamous gay or lesbian couple on a significantly higher level than familial relationships between several people in which the parameters of sexual expression are described in a way which confuses and alienates the judgmental eye of the hetero-patriarchal observer. As much as the gay person as such poses a threat to the dominating sexuality of the heterosexual man—fear of becoming overpowered, loathing already at the imagination that one may become a "bottom,"—so the diffusion perceived in lesbian and gay familial relationships alienates the non-gay patriarchically defined world into extreme reluctance toward extending legitimacy and acceptance of such relationships. Feelings of alienation with regard to lesbian and gay familial relationships are not limited, however, to the possible absence of the hetero-monogamous ideal of sexual exclusiveness.

Also the redefinition of roles played in such alternative relationships creates a head-ache to the hetero world. It remains unclear to the outside world what kind of role distribution is going on in lesbian and gay families, who is responsible for what aspects of joint life, and who is ultimately the person with decision making power. One of the most common questions asked by straight folk unfamiliar with gay people at all or at least unfamiliar with the varieties of gay coupledom is: "Who is the man and who is the woman in the relationship?"

Despite the fact that responsibilities also in a heterosexual family environment cannot in all cases be deduced exclusively from its patriarchal heterosexual structural components—whoever is on top in bed makes the decisions—the hetero-defined world imposes its warped and perverted image of the dynamics of gay sexuality onto our family relationships. Again, it remains largely unclear to the dominant heterosexual world how our relationships of love and affection, eroticism and sex, mutuality and support actually work.

4. A Proposal for Familial Relationships of Justice

Gay and lesbian families do not exist in a void, divorced from the actual people who make up such relationship. Lest we forget, gays and lesbians are real human beings with all the desires and wants, qualities and inadequacies of human beings. If they choose to engage themselves in relationships with other "real human" lesbians and gays, they expect to be treated with the same kind of dignity and respect that is advanced to all human beings. In other words, lesbian and gay familial relationships do not and cannot exist in an ethical void. Because they do not allow for themselves to be subsumed into any hetero-defined patterns of relationships, does not mean that their formation as alternatives and in opposition to hetero family structures provides them with a *carte blanche* for radically libertinist behavior which would receive its ethical legitimization by the sheer fact of its existence. Not just everything that is described as lesbian or gay family, is therefore also ethical.

In her recent book *Fierce Tenderness: A Feminist Theology of Friendship,*[14] Mary Hunt examines the conditions of contingency for friendship among women. In the central chapter of her book she introduces a "Model for 'Right Relation'"[15] in women's friendships which, in my opinion, can be assimilated with relative ease to gay and lesbian families and familial relationships. Hunt immediately alerts us to the fact that what she proposes is designed to be a model, nothing more but also nothing less. It is something to be experimented with and which, if necessity arises, is subject to change. In her interpretation the model for "right relation" is appropriate for a feminist theological interpretation of women's friendships:

> Model making is an important form of feminist theological discourse. It is a way of presenting a schema or an outline that is a heuristic device, something that helps in the learning process. It is not a magic formula for making things so. Nor is it a way to confine or limit experiences. It simply helps out in the search for ways to live in right relation by clarifying and pulling together various elements.[16]

At the heart of the model for "right relation" are four elements, namely love, power, embodiment, and spirituality. In a sketch included in the chapter, Hunt portrays the multiple relationships among these four elements in the geometrical form of a sphere, a very appropriate way of presenting these elements. The surface of a sphere has no beginning and no end. No matter where on the surface you find yourself located, you are always in the center and everything else is at once surrounding you and in intricate connection with you.

It seems to me that the geometrical description of her model as a sphere makes particular sense because .it takes appropriate care of the multiple forms of interconnectedness of the elements of friendship. Each element is connected to the other elements is a reciprocal way. The *perichoresis* of all elements on the surface of the friendship sphere prevents the possibility that one element assumes controlling power over the others. The spherical structure keeps everything in balance. If balance on the surface of the sphere is lost the entire model for friendship experiences disintegration.

In brief placative sentences which she calls "working definitions" Hunt describes what is her quintessential understanding of the four ideal constitutive elements involved in women friendships:

a. Love:

> *Love is an orientation toward the world as if my friend and I were more united than separated, more at one among the many than separate and alone....* Love is the commitment to deepen in unity without losing the uniqueness of the individuals at hand.[17]

Gay families need the strong qualitative presence of *love* in order to establish themselves as communities which are carried by more than fleeting attraction and desires for quick sexual fixes which so often invade our daily lives on the street, at work, or during periods of leisure activities. Love pulls the members of the gay familial relationship together, makes them bond deeply but at the same time does not allow for the pressures of (enforced) unity to overpower each member's sustaining individuality.

b. Power:

> *Power is the ability to make choices for ourselves, for our dependent children, and with our community....* Friendship is that relationship in which empowerment and relinquishment are most likely to take place. It is the setting in which the exchange of power and the transformation of power dynamics will be stimulated. Equally, friendships often come to an abrupt halt when power differences go unrecognized, unchallenged, and finally unchanged.[18]

It is important to note here that Hunt distinguishes between social/structural power dynamics and the manifestations of power dynamics in the personal/individual realm. The complexity of both kinds of power dynamics is intensified by their multiple modes of interaction. Empowering power for individuals and communities will have to be clearly identified as community creating and sustaining, whereas exploitative, abusive power is relationship destructive. Both, empowering as well as abusive power, can be encountered in personal/individual and in social/structural manifestations of power.

c. Embodiment:

> [Embodiment] refers to the fact that *virtually everything we do and who we are is mediated by our bodies.*[19]

What we are as human beings, as gay and lesbian human beings, we are with our bodies, unseparated and indivisible from our mental/intellectual capacities. Western religious traditions, Christianity in particular, have an indecent history of denial of the physical self. Hunt rightfully remarks that this disembodiment, religiously inspired and traditionally maintained, had detrimental effects on women's lives and their social ability to enter bonds of friendship which were recognized as authentic friendships, in a serious manner, by the dominant patriarchal tradition.

Analogized to the gay family this means that gays need to cultivate an understanding of bodiliness which transcends the barriers erected by sheer physicality. Sexual-physical expression of love for a member or the members of a gay family, for example, has to develop into more than another exercise in skillful athletics, sometimes enhanced by olfactory or tactile paraphernalia, smokes and ropes. As important as these expressions of raunchy physicality may be—and I am probably one of the last ones to deny their appropriateness—the gay family cannot allow itself to regard them as ends in themselves, without imbeddedness in relationships guided by mutuality and reciprocity, however this is to be defined in individual cases.

In the era of AIDS embodiment may—at times— have a disconcerting ring to it. But if we, as individuals and members of gay familial relationships, recognize that our being in the world with others, together with whom we experience, care for, and share the world, includes participation as psycho-physical existences, we may be able to confront the AIDS health pandemic in a responsible, *pro-active* way, in a way which does not initiate a renaissance of body denying and physicality bedeviling religious hetero-dictatorship. Claiming our bodies and their intrinsic values for ourselves means claiming our lives. Because of the history of challenge to their reproductive rights, women are at an epistemological advantage. They have already developed a more refined understanding of this issue.

d. Spirituality:

> [Spirituality] means *making choices about the quality of life for oneself and for one's community.*[20]

For Hunt this definition of spirituality

> is attention to the many options that exist to influence the way in which we live regardless of how long we live. It is attention to quality, not quantity.[21]

Gay families, perhaps more so than hetero-defined families, need to give expression to their own spirituality. Experiencing themselves under relatively constant attack from the non-gay world, quality of life decisions achieve a different sense of urgency. How do we live, how do we love, how do we relax, and also how do we die? These are questions demanding answers which can only be generated under assistance of "religion," not *any* religion, but *our* religion. What is it that belongs to that treasure we call our faith?

5. Conclusion

It may take too much to define everything that may be part of our faith treasure, however, mutuality, reciprocity, concern for the world, for others and for ourselves are integral parts of it. In whatever types of relations we are involved, concern for relational justice has to be the most significant gay family value.

Relational justice as a significant component of our spirituality sets us critically apart from the ethics of family and its values in the hetero, capitalist dominated world. In that world the focus is on a narrow interpretation of relationships in the biogenetically defined family without attempting to establish a micro-family transcending perspective.

Yes, it may be very true that gay family is what we—based on our own pluriform family experiences—define as *our gay* family. It may be inclusive of modes of behavior with which we, at times, are perhaps uncomfortable. As long as our ways of being in relationships in the world are under the guidance of our spiritual maxim of relational justice and follow an ethics of concern for all of creation we have neither reason nor right to be anathematizingly judgmental of our sisters and brothers. The real bonus of this discussion of family, ethics, and values lies, from my perspective, in the fact that an expanded understanding of gay familial relationships takes attention away from narrowly focusing on biogenetic relationships and on physical sexual expression within the confines of legally recognized marriages as their singular legitimizing agency.

1 Meanwhile I was informed through knowledgable sources that the child has been named Avery.

2 See Paulo Freire, *The Pedagogy of the Oppressed* (New York, NY: Continuum, 1978).

3 Kath Weston, *Families We Choose: Lesbians, Gays, Kinship* (New York, NY: Columbia University Press, 1991).

4 Ibid., p. 1.

5 Ibid., p. 2.

6 Ibid., p. 3.

7 Ibid., p. 56.

8 "Toward a Unified Analysis of Gender and Kinship," in Jane F. Collier and Sylvia J. Yanagisako, eds., *Gender and Kinship: Essays Toward a Unified Analysis* (Stanford, CA: Stanford University Press, 1987), pp. 14-50.

9 Weston, p. 2.

10 Ibid., p. 3.

11 Ibid., p. 5.

12 See J. Michael Clark's remarks on long term committed gay and lesbian couples and their surrogate family networks in his review of Kath Weston's book *Families We Choose: Lesbians, Gays, Kinship* in Michael L. Stemmeler and J. Michael Clark, eds., *Gay Affirmative Ethics* (Las Colinas, TX: Monument Press, 1993), pp. 125-129.

13 See also J. Michael Clark, ibid., p. 126.

14 Mary E. Hunt, *Fierce Tenderness: A Feminist Theology of Friendship* (New York, NY: Crossroad, 1991).

15 See *Fierce Tendernes,* chapter 4: "Fierce Tenderness: A Model for 'Right Relation.'"

16 Hunt, p. 90.

17 Ibid., p. 100.

18 Ibid., pp. 101-102.

19 Ibid., p. 102.

20 Ibid., p. 105.

21 Ibid., p. 105.

IV. Mark R. Kowalewski and Elizabeth A. Say:

Lesbian and Gay Family: Iconoclasm and Reconstruction

1. Preface

During the 1992 Presidential campaign, the term "family values" exploded onto the political scene as a battle cry for conservative ideology. However, it was clear to us that when Dan Quayle championed the American family, he did not include us in his ideal vision. In fact, it was often difficult to know who precisely he was talking about, since he neglected to specify to which family and to whose values he referred. He got away with this because there is an unspoken assumption about family in this country, that all families are Euro-American, middle-class, and, most importantly, heterosexual. While we are middle-class, Euro-Americans, we remain margi-nalized. Where were we to fit, a gay man and a lesbian, in Dan Quayle's idealized picture of family life?

This paper is our attempt to address this question; to explain why we are absent, and to suggest ways in which we may write ourselves into a new vision of family. In doing so, we hope also to suggest a re-defining of values that can serve to strengthen and support the multiplicity of changing family structures which exist in American society.

2. Introduction

It was the fall of 1982. I stood with my father at the top of a low hill, looking down at the small Pennsylvania farm that had been in his family for over 150 years. My great Aunt had just died, the last of her generation, and we had come to close up the house and prepare the farm for sale. It was an emotionally exhausting time for my father, as he said farewell to his past. He put his arm around my shoulders and said "Family is everything. It's all that really matters."

I've thought about those words often in the past ten years, as my immediate family has gone through changes wrought by marriage, children, divorce. For my father, family is everything. He was an only child, and lived a relatively lonely childhood in the company, primarily, of adults. When he married, my mother and the six children they raised together became the center of his life. My childhood conformed to the 1950s stereotype of idyllic American family life, and it was not until I reached my teens that I began to understand that we were the exception and not the rule.

It was about the same time that I began to come into conflict with my family. They were religiously and politically conservative and I was in the full flower of youthful rebellion. Fortunately, my younger brother followed in my footsteps and I had at least one ally in the frequently heated debates that became part of the dinner hour. Nevertheless, the arguments were painful and I was often torn by conflicting emotions of guilt and disappointment. Guilt because I was the source of familial turmoil and disappointment because I felt that

> *I had been betrayed by those from whom I expected support. (Beth)*

The icon of the American family holds forth promises that are unrealistic and problematic. It promises to be all things, to meet all needs, to provide a safe haven of unconditional support and acceptance. The family has been idealized to such an extent that, in comparison, all other relationships are viewed as secondary and inferior.

> *Several years ago I had a conversation with a woman in her mid-fifties who complained that she felt bored and lonely now that her children had grown up and moved out. I suggested she get involved in some new activities and make some friends. She responded in anger "I have a husband and six children—I shouldn't have to make friends!" (Beth)*

> Friends are who you pass pleasant time with, who you like but don't love, to whom you make minimal if any commitment... Friends, in that most demeaning of phrases, are "just friends." And we have believed it; we have mystified it and mythologized it. We have taken the lie for the truth, and in doing so we have almost made it true.[1]

As Michéle Barrett and Mary McIntosh argue, in *The Anti-social Family,*[2] this mythologized family has been elevated above all other social institutions as the place where our affective needs will be met and satisfied. This is the seduction of the myth, and the reason it continues to hold sway despite the fact that it fails to deliver on the promise more often than not. "If the family were not the only source of a range of satisfactions, were it not so massively privileged, it would not be so attractive."[3]

This is precisely what makes the myth such a powerful image in public rhetoric. One need only intone the words "The Family" to evoke an emotional response from an audience. There is no need to specify which family, whose family, is being referred to; there is no need to put content to the concept. Indeed, were one to attempt to specify the content, the myth would be difficult to maintain.

> *As a child I had an image of what a family should be, partly informed by television idealizations and partly from my Catholic school education where the Holy Family was set forth as the romanticized ideal. My family experience, however, did not mirror Mary, Joseph, and Jesus at home in Nazareth. A frequently absent and alcoholic father characterized my home life. When he came home my mother would complain about why he came home so late, they would argue, then he would usually fall asleep—after eating a warmed-over dinner. (Mark)*

Karen Lindsey poses the question "When *was* the Golden Age of the happy family?"[4] The myth, she argues, ignores the history of abusive family relationships, and ignores the fact that while the family may have been a refuge for the husband/father, this was frequently not the case for wives and children. The myth also fails to acknowledge the fact that, historically, persons entered into family structures out of necessity rather than choice, and it frequently became an inescapable prison.[5]

Furthermore, numbers of Americans living outside of traditional families have increased in recent decades. "Non-family Households," which include any persons not related by consanguinity or marriage, increased from 15% of all households in 1960, to

26% in 1980, and 29% in 1990.[6] Males who never married increased from 19% of the U.S. male population over eighteen years of age in 1970, to 24% in 1980, to 26% in 1989. During the same time period never-married females increased from 14% in 1970 to 17% in 1980, to 19% in 1989.[7] While increasing numbers of Americans do not live in traditional family structures, the unchallenged acceptance of the idealized family precludes a thoroughgoing critique of it.

In fact, as Barrett and McIntosh argue, "the family" is a socially constructed unit that purports to explain how people live together in society. As such, the concept of family is subject to disagreement as to its actual meaning.[8] Nevertheless, this ideal of family is seen as inevitable, "...as a biological unit rather than a social arrangement."[9] This echoes the claim made by Kath Weston that "the American Family" is a contested concept which must be understood in the context of power relations within society.[10]

3. Family Values

What, then, are these "family values" which became the call to arms during the presidential election campaign? We discuss five elements composing the core of the ideal of family in the United States: fidelity, generation/renewal, unconditional love, duty/obligation, and the family as source of identity and community. We would agree that each of these constitutes a value in and of itself. Nevertheless, we disagree with the particular construction of these values by the dominant, heterosexist culture.

a. Fidelity

Heterosexual marital monogamy is the primary value, not only because it is the necessary precondition for maintaining the dominant cultural model, but also because all family values which follow become perversions when exercised apart from this. This value is reinforced by both religious and political institutions in the United States.

Yoel H. Kahn has noted that, within traditional Judaism, the halachic norms establish that sexual relations between opposite sex-partners, within the context of marriage, is the only "licit and sacred" form of sexual expression.[11] The same can be said of Roman Catholic teachings on sexuality. Although the Second Vatican Council resulted in a change in attitude toward human sexuality, and affirmed the good of sexual relations, this good exists only within heterosexual marriage.[12] Paul VI, in *Humane Vitae*, promulgated in 1967, states that Christian marriage has two ends. One is as an expression of the love of the two partners, but this must result in openness to children. Since progeny is an end of marriage, it is essential that Christian marriage can only be heterosexual. In both Jewish and Christian traditions, legitimate sexual expression is act centered, rather than relation centered. Individuals with complementary gender (i.e. male and female) engage in sexual acts which lead potentially to procreation. Any sexual act outside these boundaries is not only morally inferior, but a perversion of human nature itself.

James B. Nelson, commenting on traditional norms within Protestantism, states that the notion of "co-humanity" (the complimentary necessity of men and women) results in the suggestion that full human existence is possible only within heterosexual marriage.[13] We find this notion reflected in a "homespun" marriage manual from the late nineteenth century.

> Marriage...is God's own ideal of completeness. It was when he saw that it was not good for man to be alone that woman

was made and brought to him to supply
what was lacking.[14]

Furthermore, the author asserts:

> It is not by accident that men live in fami-
> lies rather than solitarily. The human race
> began in a family, and Eden was a home.
> The divine blessing has ever rested upon
> nations and communities just in the mea-
> sure in which they have adhered to these
> original institutions and have kept mar-
> riage and the home pure and holy; and
> blight and curse have come just in the
> measure in which they have departed from
> these divine models, dishonoring marriage
> and tearing down the sacred walls of
> home.[15]

It is this concept of marriage and the family that Pat
Robertson seemed to have in mind when he spoke at
the Republican convention. It was there that he
(among others) attacked any suggestion that alternative family structures were legitimate. "When Bill
and Hillary Clinton talk about family values, they are
not talking about either families or values. They are
talking about a radical plan to destroy the traditional
family...."[16]   This religious privileging of heterosexual marriage is legitimated in civil law, evidenced
by the fact that the only relationships that receive legal sanction and support are heterosexual ones.

b. *Generation/renewal*

Once securely married, the next family value is
progeny. Those who marry and do not raise children
are suspect, often suffering the accusation of selfishness or, even worse, refusing to grow up. Again, this
value is given religious and political sanction. Within

Roman Catholic moral teaching, the dominant view, for centuries, was that procreation was the "natural purpose or end of sexual expression."[17] As late as the 1950s, with the Papal document *Casti Connubii*, procreation was seen as the only legitimate end of sexual relations within marriage. Kahn notes that the halachah has "an overwhelming bias towards procreation," and that generally only "...sexual acts which are *presumably* procreative [are] licit."[18] James Nelson argues that although Protestantism broke with the Catholic teaching that procreation was the primary purpose of sexual relations, it has nevertheless given a normative religious status to the nuclear family.[19] Within American Protestantism there was, in the early twentieth century, "...a strong emphasis on the duty of Protestant families to procreate abundantly in order to stem the dilution of [their] religious dominance by the increasing waves of Catholic immigration."[20]

Both political liberals and conservatives espouse their commitment to children. Conservative rhetoric, of course, focuses on the so-called "Pro-Life" position that claims to champion the lives of unborn children. Among liberals, the pro-child position is reflected in commitment to social policies which provide economic and political support to children, such as AFDC, or the Family Leave Bill.

Furthermore, generation/renewal is a central family value not only because it assures the production of children and the continuing of biological lineage, but is the means by which the traditional notion of family is reproduced. Children are socialized to accept traditional family values and often traditional gender roles associated with those values. Thus, the continuance of the ideological lineage is assured as well.

c. Unconditional love, duty/obligation

According to the myth of the family, once the family unit is established there are further values that govern the interaction of family members. The next two of these we have chosen to discuss together because, although they are separate, they are nevertheless mutually reinforcing: Unconditional Love and Duty/Obligation.[21] These are well represented in the hackneyed phrase "Blood is thicker than water." On the one hand this suggests unquestioned support from one's family members, no matter what. But, at the same time, it also requires absolute prior loyalty to blood kin over and above all other relationships one may have.

The assumption that the family provides unconditional love and acceptance is perhaps one of the most seductive aspects of the idealized family.

> [E]ach of us needs a place where the gifts of life make us more human, where we are linked with ongoing covenants to others, where we can return to lick our wounds, where we can take our shoes off, and where we know that—within the bounds of human capacity—we are loved simply because we *are*.[22]

In return for the promised unconditional love, family members (especially children) are supposed to recognize that they have a duty and obligation to the family. Within the Judeo-Christian tradition the injunction to "Honor your father and your mother" has frequently been used as a proof text to support the notion of familial duty and obligation.

I remember when I was growing up that, whenever I had an argument with my parents that reached an unresolvable point they would pull this commandment out like a trump card.

*"But why do I have to do this, that, or the
other thing?" I would demand. "Give me one
good reason why." "Because," they would
intone, "the Bible says you should honor
your mother and father." There was never
any acceptable response to this except acqui-
escence. (Beth)*

d. Identity and community

Finally, the myth of the family promises a sense of
identity and belonging. That this is so is taken for
granted in most discussions about family, rather than
argued for or against. Barrett and McIntosh note that
all aspects of social life are planned on the assumption that people live in traditional families. "Those
who do not are isolated and deprived."[23]

Within the myth of the family, relationality is defined primarily in genealogical or biological terms.
This is assumed in such things as inheritance laws
and the right of the "next of kin" to make decisions
about health care for a loved one unless other arrangements have been legally specified. Embedded in
familial relations are other aspects of identity and
belonging, such as ethnic and/or religious ties. So, we
identify ourselves as Irish-Catholic, Southern-Baptist,
Jewish, etc. To choose a marriage partner outside of
the community has frequently been seen as a betrayal
of one's family.

An interesting contemporary twist on this has
been the recent emphasis on adopted children locating their "real" (read: biological) parents. As a society we provide mixed messages about who is family:
we legitimize chosen families through legal adoption,
while at the same time providing a subtext that im-
plies there is something lacking in these arrangements.[24]

4. Iconoclasm

a. Fidelity

In her now classic essay, "Compulsory Heterosexuality and Lesbian Existence," Adrienne Rich succinctly demonstrated the ways in which society works to ensure heterosexual privilege in our society.[25] Rich challenges the presumed givenness of heterosexual marriage as the natural form of human affective relationships, suggesting that "heterosexuality, like motherhood, needs to be recognized and studied as a *political institution.*"[26]

As Rich further clarifies, heterosexual privilege reinforces male privilege. The primary family value that conservatives and liberals alike espouse is the privilege of heterosexual men to control their wives and children. This was never so evident as when Dan Quayle condemned Murphy Brown for bearing a child out of wedlock (the term wedlock is itself revealing[27]). By doing so she had, in Quayle's words, "mocked the importance of fathers." What disturbed the Vice-President was not that she had born a child, but that she had done so independent of male control. Clearly, in Quayle's viewpoint, if there is no father present there is no family unit.

> [T]he failure to examine heterosexuality as an institution is like failing to admit that the economic system called capitalism or the caste system of racism is maintained by a variety of forces, including both physical violence and false consciousness.[28]

Despite the fact that popular rhetoric presupposes a Golden Age of the family, as Lindsey points out there is little historical evidence to support it. Contemporary statistics emphasize the fact that the traditional family is as likely to be a place of violence and abuse as it is to be a place of love and support. It is estimated that between one-third and one-half of all women who live with a male partner will experience brutality or the threat of brutality from this man who is supposed to love them. Forty-one percent of all female homicides are women who are killed by their husbands.[29]

According to Okin, heterosexual marriage, as we have known it, works to make and keep women vulnerable because the myth of the family ignores the power dynamics within families.

> Gender-structured marriage is a clear case of socially created and reinforced inequality... [F]or many centuries marriage has been the paradigmatic contract between unequals, operating so as to accentuate and deepen the initial inequality.[30]

Power, as an issue of justice, has been critiqued in terms of its public manifestations but ignored in relation to the family because the family is seen as a private institution, beyond the realm of appropriate state intervention. However, as Okin points out, the state does, in fact, intrude on the family in numerous ways. Family law has historically worked to enforce the rights of husbands and fathers. The law has also served to make women economically dependent on men by legally denying to women rights enjoyed by men in the workplace.[31]

Given the fact that marriage is so clearly a bastion of male privilege, and male privilege so much a given in our culture, anyone who refuses to participate in heterosexual marriage does, in a very real sense, threaten the very fabric of our society. Homosexual relationships may be understood as an alternative discourse that challenges not only the presumed givenness of heterosexuality, but also the corresponding power relations. According to Sarah

Lucia Hoagland, heterosexualism is a way of living
that "...normalizes the dominance of one person in a
relationship and the subordination of another."[32]
Thus, she claims that her goal is not moral reform
(bringing actions into conformity with accepted
principles), but rather is moral revolution (the creation
of new values).[33]

b. Generation/renewal

Despite the fact that almost every politician pays lip
service to the importance of children, our public
record on providing for the health and well being of
children is abysmal: "Every eight seconds of the
school day, a child drops out. Every 26 seconds of
each day, a child runs away from home....Every 7
minutes a child is arrested for a drug offense. Every
day, 100,000 children are homeless....Every 53
minutes, a child dies due to poverty."[34]

Because responsibility for child-care falls primarily to women, women's greater economic vulnerability translates into vulnerability for their children
as well. The high rate of divorce in heterosexual
marriage in recent decades is well documented; between 50 and 60 percent of all children born in the
1980's are expected to be children of divorce before
they are eighteen.[35] As Okin points out, "...the economic costs of divorce fall overwhelmingly on
women and children, and not on men."[36] Thus, despite the public rhetoric about commitment to children, women and their children make up a dispro-
portionate number of those who live under the
poverty level.

Children being raised in households without both
parents present has increased since 1970. Women
householders raising children moved from 10% of all
households with children in 1970 to 20% in 1989.
Male householders with children increased from 1%
to 3% in the same time period.[37]

Given the presumption of heterosexual marriage, it becomes clear that, if children are valued, it is only within the context of certain kinds of relationships. Since the concept of family is predicated on a heterosexual norm, most straight people find it difficult to conceive of childbearing outside of this configuration. According to Weston, one of the major concerns expressed by parents of lesbians and gays, when confronted with their child's sexuality, is that there will be no grandchildren. The assumption is simply that being homosexual precludes the possibility of children.[38] If lesbians and gays have children, there are additional problems because this is seen as a perversion of the natural order of things. The stories of lesbians and gay men being denied custody of their biological children, or having their custody rights severely restricted, are legion. Thus, lesbians and gay men with minor children often feel it necessary to conceal their sexuality, further reinforcing the misconception that homosexuals are not parents.

> Being the child in a gay family, for me, meant telling lies. My mother asked me not to tell my friends that she was gay, comparing the embarrassment to a secret we shared about an eraser I had once stolen from a stationery store. There was little danger that I would say anything.[39]

Even if straight people can imagine lesbian and gay parents, there is a general assumption that this is unhealthy for the children. As Weston points out, during the 1980s the Presidential Task Force on Adoption recommended against allowing homosexuals to become adoptive parents. At the same time, foster care policy became more restrictive, and lesbians and gay men were assigned to the status of "parents of last resort."[40]

I recall a couple of years ago entertaining the possibility of becoming a father. Straight friends sometimes asked whether I really thought this idea would be good for the child. What would it be like to grow up in a gay family? When I think back now, I wonder why they didn't wonder equally what it was like to grow up gay in a straight family? (Mark)

c. Unconditional love, duty/obligation

As many lesbians and gay men have discovered, familial love is indeed conditional. It can be, and often is, withdrawn if one does not fulfill the obligations of the dutiful daughter or son. These obligations are more often than not constructed around a heterosexual norm. "Coming out to a biological relative puts to the test the unconditional love and enduring solidarity commonly understood in the United States to characterize blood ties."[41]

This is, at least in part, due to the assumption that the heterosexual family is defined by nature/biology, rather than by voluntary participation or choice. Thus, when the lesbian or gay man chooses an option other than heterosexuality they are accused of destroying the family. As Hoagland argues, hetero-patriarchy "...cannot afford to acknowledge that participation is a choice."[42] By not fulfilling one's obligation to the biological family (conforming to the expectations of the heterosexual norm), one forfeits the right to unconditional love. Within the patriarchal value system, argues Hoagland, obedience becomes the primary moral virtue, reinforced by both religion and culture.[43] The notion of obedience carries with it, at least implicitly, the demand for self-sacrifice. After all, if obedience is required, it must be expected that one will occasionally have to sacrifice her own desires out of obedience to the patriarchal authority.

However, in inequitable power relations, says Hoagland, "...altruism accrues to the one in the subordinate position."[44] She goes on to say that "selfishness" is a label given to people who refuse to "go along with the group," and is used to "manipulate our participation toward someone else's end."[45]

In a television interview, George Bush was asked how he would respond if one of his grandchildren were to announce that she/he were homosexual. Bush began by saying he would put his arms around that grandchild, and love him. But then he went on to say that he hoped that this person would not go out and promote a homosexual lifestyle as normal; that this person would not become an advocate for homosexual marriages or homosexual rights.[46] Clearly the love is conditional on the grandchild sacrificing his own interests to those of his more powerful grandfather.

It is not only homosexual children who discover the conditional nature of familial love and support; any transgression of one's duty to family can cause a breach in the relationship.

> *A friend of mine was raised as the only daughter in a very close-knit Jewish family. As such she was completely doted on, the darling of her parents. That is, until she eloped and married an African-American man. Suddenly, the love and support which she had come to expect was withdrawn. She had betrayed her parents, and they quite literally cut her off. Things are better now, several years later, but the level of trust will never be the same again. (Beth)*

d. *Identity and community*

Here again, as many lesbians and gay men know, coming to terms with one's own sexual identity frequently means a severing of familial identity. Weston notes that after the experience of coming out, often including a long process of self-discovery, many lesbians and gay men also discover a change in their relations with biological family members. "When I tell you 'who I (really) am," she states, "I find out who you (really) are to me."[47]

If we begin with the premise that our society is structured around the norm of the heterosexual family, that this model of family is privileged religiously, socially, politically, and economically, it is safe to assume that when one withdraws from it, such withdrawal is accompanied by severe cost. To openly identify oneself as lesbian or gay is to become vulnerable. The lesbian or gay person must face the real possibility that she/he may lose employment, or find custody rights even to biological children withdrawn. They live with the knowledge that their relationships will have no legal standing or protection, and little or no social acceptance. They know that their choice to love a person of the same sex makes them a target for verbal and physical abuse.

They must face, as well, the very real possibility that "coming out" will mean the severing of ties with blood kin. It will mean the loss of that sense of identity and belonging which is so much a part of our psychological make-up. Jungian psychoanalytic theory, in relation to myth, has claimed that, for women, marriage has been a kind of death; the woman dies to her old identity as she assumes a new identity as a wife, an identity defined in relation to her husband.[48] Similarly, the lesbian or gay person must also die to a past identity. Unfortunately, there is no socially sanctioned new identity to which she/he may be reborn.

5. *Whose Family? Whose Values?*

Despite all the rhetoric about family values, upon closer inspection we discover that these values are narrow, restrictive, and privilege only one family ideal over all other possibilities: the heterosexual male-dominated family. And even within this model, the reality frequently fails to deliver on all that the myth promises.

> The family may well have been—and may well still be—a "haven from the heartless world" for many men. But for women and children, it has always been the very *center* of the heartless world, from which no haven existed.[49]

It has become abundantly clear in recent years that domestic violence has reached epidemic proportions in the United States. Battery is the single major cause of injury to women, more significant than street rape, muggings, or auto accidents.[50] According to a survey of battered women, more than 75% of these women reported that their children had been physically or sexually abused by their batterers.[51] Thus, the notion that the family is a place of love and protection is specious, at best.

Nevertheless, the hegemony enjoyed by the myth of the family provides only two alternatives. Either one lives within the boundaries of the mythic construction of family, or one has no family at all. There are no other options available within the dominant culture.

> The acceptance of these alternatives as the parameters of human experience leaves us little real choice. If we wish to retain our humanity—to be caring, nurturing people and, by the same token, cared-for and nurtured people—we must opt for the

traditional family. Whatever evils we
perceive in the nuclear family, the freedom
to live without human relationships is
ultimately no freedom, but hell.[52]

The accepted givenness of this model of family ex-
cludes any alternative notions of family from the language of familial relations. Persons may live in other
types of relationships, but these are not family. When
Kath Weston, and others, speak of "families we
choose" they undertake iconoclasm, shattering the
myth of the status quo.

The assumption made by heterosexual society is
that, as Weston points out, "Straight" is to "Gay"
as "Family" is to "No Family". If one does not fit
within the parameters provided by the traditional
heterosexual nuclear family, then of course she will
live in isolation. As one lesbian reported to Kath
Weston, her mother had warned her: "'You'll be a
lesbian and you'll be alone the rest of your life. Even
a dog shouldn't be alone.'"[53]

Problematically, when we attempt to create alternative family structures to ward off such dire predic-
tions, we are given no social, economic or political
support. According to Beverly Harrison, society is
shaped by two mutually reinforcing social systems,
the productive and the reproductive.[54] The degree to
which one fits into this structure will determine the
support one derives from it. As noted, given the
construction of the family as the heterosexual nuclear
family, lesbians and gays do not fit into the reproductive system as it exists. Furthermore, our failure to
fit into this system is seen as a failure of lesbians and
gay men, not a failure of the system itself.

Since the productive system is premised on this
same heterosexual norm, lesbians and gays are also
marginalized in this area. The distribution of insurance benefits is simply one example: since homosexual relationships (and other non-state sanctioned
partnerships) are not recognized as family relation-

ships by most companies, a lesbian cannot secure these benefits for her partner or her partner's children. This places additional financial hardship on someone who is already more at risk economically due to heterosexist values in the workplace.

As Okin notes, corporate America is structured in such a way that it assumes its workers have a wife at home.[55] A gay man cannot apply for paternity leave if he or his partner were to adopt a child since, according to the dominant definition, he is not a father. Paternity leave is rare, even for heterosexual men, and as Okin observes, men who want to be actively involved in child rearing will find their career goals compromised.[56] This is, of course, because child-rearing is seen as "women's work". Heteropatriarchy privileges the productive role of men in the public sphere. Thus, any man who gives up that privilege to participate in the more despised "women's sphere" (home and family) is suspect. As Harrison asserts, "Our real problem—the moral one—is that we have a social system that cannot accommodate the well-being of real, living people, a system that shunts people aside if they do not 'fit' *its* needs."[57] Thus the message becomes clear. Not only does our society warn that we will be alone, it works to insure this will be so—punishment for having the audacity to violate the rules.

6. *Reconstruction*

Given the critique of values we have engaged in thus far, we make some tentative steps in reconstructing values we believe may be embraced by gays and lesbians. We believe these are grounded in the experiences of many, but certainly not all, gay and lesbian people. We see the values we discuss here as jumping-off points, as places where playful discourse may emerge.

FIGURE ONE

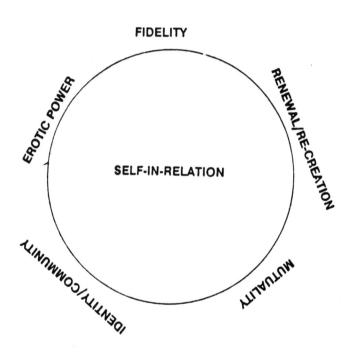

DIALECTIC OF FAMILY VALUES

Figure one displays the values we set forth. Lesbian/gay family values include: fidelity, renewal/re-creation, mutuality, identity/community, and erotic power. Each of these values is related to the others. The circular shape of the model indicates the reciprocal nature of these values. If we consider the circle to be a dynamic model then the values we discuss may be understood to be in creative tension with each other. The self-in-relation, in the context of the family/community, is at the center of the circle to illustrate that these values serve the good of persons and communities, that they foster their flourishing. When such values become a burden and destroy human well-being then they should be discarded. Any group of values is always historically bound and constructed in the context of experience. Thus, we cannot hold values or principles to be absolute and unchanging.

a. Fidelity

Within traditionalist moral discourse fidelity is often narrowly bound to the idea of sexual exclusivity. That is, a moral sexual act takes place only within the boundaries of the marital understanding of fidelity. Faithfulness goes beyond this narrow definition. We agree with Jim Cotter when he states:

> To be 'faithful' is to be 'full of faith', full of trust, to be willing to let love be vulnerable. Only so can love create love, can the commitment be creative.[58]

This understanding of fidelity is not focused on the sexual act, but on the total context of the relationship between persons who trust and love one another. Indeed, faithfulness within the biblical traditions rests on the context of a relationship. For example, in the Prophetic tradition, divine love is evidenced through a history of relationship. Faithfulness is tied to remembrance, a recollection of a history of relationship demonstrated through concrete experiences. Conversely, faithlessness and forgetfulness are deemed as sinful because they deny what has taken place between people and between people and God over time. In this understanding of fidelity, our relationships are forged over time through acts where love is made incarnate. In turn, loving actions reinforce the significance of those relationships for us.

Sexual acts are part of this larger framework of fidelity. I can trust you sexually because I have a relationship with you. I can be vulnerable to you because we have a shared history wherein I know it is safe to be with you. Nevertheless, sex is only one area in which fidelity in primary relationships is expressed. The entire loving relationship is reinforced by continued concrete expressions of love on a daily basis. This, in fact, is what it means to "make love."

Sexual expressions between partners may also be a symbolic expression of fidelity and of the uniqueness of a particular relationship. Yet, the symbolic nature of monogamy must be negotiated between the partners. In an ethic based on context rather than absolute norms, such as we advocate, it is possible that sexual sharing beyond the confines of the primary partnership may be morally acceptable in some relationships.

The broader context of fidelity also expands the concept to include relations with other members of our gay/lesbian families. These too are created over time. Our history with each other continues to build our relationships and reinforces that which already exits.

b. *Renewal/re-creation*

While renewing the family through procreation is a value within the heterosexist model of family, gays and lesbians have also been parents. Lesbians and gays have either assumed parenthood through choices they made earlier in life (in heterosexual unions), or through choices they have made since they have "come out" (generally by utilizing reproductive technologies). The option of producing or raising children is an option gays and lesbians should value.

The atmosphere of a gay family may be as nurturing as a family in which the parents are differently gendered, perhaps more so. The extended family networks of lesbians, for example, may provide a rich context for rearing children. In a study of lesbian mothers, Julie Ainslie and Kathryn Felty note that the women they interviewed believed they were helping form a new generation with feminist values in which each individual is seen as unique in her/himself and not restricted by narrow role choices and definitions so often found in traditional families. Moreover, these women saw their lesbian families as helping to recreate and redefine the notion of family.[59]

> *Recently, at an academic conference a gay friend of mine pulled out a photograph of himself, a woman and a small child. On the face of it they were the picture of the "normal" family. Yet the picture represented a lesbian who had a child through artificial insemination with a gay man. The child would be raised by her mother and her partner and my friend. He commented that they believed the girl would have a very loving childhood with the nurturing of two mothers and a father. (Mark)*

Creating new family structures is another aspect of the value of renewal and recreation. Lesbians and gays, often rejected because of their difference from the traditionalist family model where difference is illegitimate, have created families from friendship networks out of necessity. Yet this necessity has proven to be a virtue. The very existence of variously structured gay and lesbian families provides a prophetic example for the social reconstruction of the hegemonic ideal of family.

The notion of "wider families" also points to other family structures which challenge traditional notions and point to alternative constructions of the family. For example, Carol Stack's study of African American families challenged her traditionalist construction of *the* family. Once immersed in alternative structures her vision was broadened. She embraced a richer and more creative understanding of what constituted family.[60]

Another dimension of the value of renewal/re-creation is the renewal and re-creation of our selves in the context of our relationships with lesbian/gay family members. Families provide us with a sense of identity, they also can transform our sense of who we are for better or worse. The power of creation is the power to bring something new into being. Creativity is not simply a rejection of what has gone before, nor does it rely on originality of substance. "It is the ability to bring a new vision of existent conceptions, and to do so in a way that they become authentic for others."[61] Thus, in creativity we transcend the limits imposed by received definitions of reality; we create a new vision. Our associations with our partners and our extended families over time transform us. We are no longer the persons we were when we entered these relationships.

Furthermore, the value of hospitality is implied in the broader value of renewal/re-creation. Homes of gay and lesbian persons can be places where nurturing occurs—havens from a heartless world, places where we can be who we are, where we can be renewed and recreate. Particularly at holiday times, the hospitality of lesbian and gay friends can provide an atmosphere of caring and celebration in situations where contact with biological kin may be problematic.

We believe that the creation of homes by lesbians and gays serves as a prophetic reminder to ourselves to open our doors or our selves in hospitality to the "other," the "outsider," the stranger in our midst. This is not unlike the ancient biblical injunction to be hospitable, since all lesbians and gays have been "strangers" and "aliens" to one extent or another.

c. Mutuality

The opportunity for the creation of new family structures in the context of gay/lesbian communities also presents the opportunity to create partnerships based on mutuality rather than on the dualism of dominance and submission characteristic of hetero-patriarchy. In heterosexist families the division of labor is gender-based, as is the importance placed on the work men and women do, with men's roles and activity being valued more highly in society than women's. Certainly examples exist of lesbians and gays simply recreating the heterosexist paradigm in the gay context rather than transcending these limiting categories and creating something new. The value of mutuality recognizes that both persons are full and contributing members of the partnership with each person empowering the other.

The dominance and submission dualism is worked out sexually in the heterosexist family. Alternatively, Beverly Harrison argues for the value of mutuality as applied to sex:

> Sexual communication, at its best, mutually enhances self-respect and valuation of the other. The moral norm for sexual communication in a feminist ethic is radical mutuality—the simultaneous acknowledgment of vulnerability to the need

of another, the recognition of one's own
power to give and receive pleasure and to
call forth another's power of relation and
to express one's own.[62]

The value of mutuality is not only valid in a feminist
ethic, but we believe that this feminist value must inform relationships between gay men. Moreover,
valuing and respecting the other and also receiving
from the other, not sacrificing ourselves for the other,
should go beyond sex to impact our relationships
generally with our gay/lesbian family members.

d. *Identity and community*

We have noted above that our families of origin, as
well as our gay families help to give us our identity.
Nevertheless, we argue that community in itself forms
a value. Individuals are not selves in isolation. Rather,
we are selves in relation, born in a context of
community and socialized for good or for ill into a
community. The gay/lesbian communities of which
lesbian/gay families are a part shapes and forms us.
When we came out as gay men or lesbians we
undertook a reshaping of our identity in the context
of a community. Gay and lesbian families as well as
larger gay/lesbian communities both exist as
prophetic examples of alternative discourse, of a voice
different from that of heteropatriarchy. These
alternative discourse communities provide the larger
context for social critique and resistance to the dominant discourse. They also provide a broader context
for lesbian and gay solidarity[63] in the work for social
transformation.

e. Erotic Power

In her discussion of "erotic power," Rita Brock contrasts *agape,* disinterested or objective love, with *eros,* which she defines as:

> intimacy through subjective engagement
> of the whole self in a relationship...The
> erotic bridges the passions of our lives by
> a sensual span of physical, emotional,
> psychic, mental and spiritual elements.[64]

The erotic has too often been equated with the sexual, she notes. Rather, it is a love which is directed both to our selves and real persons to whom we are related. It is the power that connects us to embodied others. It is that force which allows us to make empathetic connections with others. Thus, the erotic is that which empowers us to have a hunger for justice in society. Yet such erotic power needs to emerge from within one's self. Only when one accepts oneself for who she/he is and gains a sense of personal empowerment can erotic power manifest itself in our lives.

Brock notes that the first place where we may feel erotic power is in our families of origin where we first feel connectedness and intimacy.[65] Yet, as we have noted above, biological families may also be the place where we feel most disconnected from ourselves and our sexuality. Our family relations may break our hearts the most. Furthermore, our gay/lesbian families may be the place in which we are renewed and restored, where erotic power is nurtured. This occurs in our most intimate partnerships, but also with our extended lesbian and gay kin. The concrete acts of love we show our gay/lesbian family members help to nurture them and renew them. Incarnate love is erotic power in action. Once again, these acts of love demonstrate the reality of our relationships, they reinforce the intimacy of gay/lesbian kinship over time. The power and the passion of erotic love is really the force guiding the other values we have articulated.

7. Conclusion

As we write our concluding thoughts it is the evening of November 3, 1992, and the Presidential election is a resounding victory for Bill Clinton. We are on the eve of a new era in American political life; one where lesbians and gay men are in the center of the political arena. Significantly, it may be our presence there that will offer real possibility for rethinking our notions of what it means to belong to a family; notions that although derived from lesbian and gay experience, have meaning for all persons who do not live in traditional families. As we have pointed out, this traditional model of family is increasingly a minority experience. If we truly are to value the American family in the future, this must include all those alternative family structures that Dan Quayle and George Bush could not envision.

1 Karen Lindsey, "Friends as Family" in Gary Colombo, Robert Cullen, Bonnie Lisle, eds., *Rereading America: Cultural Contexts for Critical Thinking and Writing.* (New York: St. Martin's Press, 1989), [pp. 398–412], p. 405.

2 Michéle Barrett and Mary McIntosh, *The Antisocial Family* (London: NLB, 1982).

3 Ibid., p. 133.

4 Lindsey, p. 401. Similar critiques are made, and dealt with in greater depth, in Susan Moller Okin, *Justice, Gender, and the Family* (Basic Books, 1989). Okin argues persuasively that the gendered-structured family is inherently unjust and serves as the training ground for all other forms of injustice in society.

5 Ibid., p. 404.

6 *United States Statistical Abstracts* (Washington, D.C.: U.S. Government Publishing Office, 1991), p. 45.

7 Ibid., p. 44.

8 Barrett and McIntosh, p. 95.

9 Ibid., p. 27.

10 Kath Weston, *Families We Choose: Lesbians, Gays, Kinship* (New York: Columbia University Press, 1991), p. 3.

11 Yoel H. Kahn, "Making Love as Making Justice: Toward a New Jewish Ethic of Sexuality," in Michael L. Stemmeler and J. Michael Clark, eds., *Gay Affirmative Ethics* (Las Colinas, TX: Monument Press, 1993), pp. 27-42.

12 Daniel C. Maguire, *The Moral Revolution* (San Francisco: Harper and Row, 1986), pp. 87-102.

13 James B. Nelson, *Between Two Gardens: Reflections on Sexuality and Religious Experience* (New York: The Pilgrim Press, 1983), p. 86.

14 Rev. J.R. Miller, D.D., *The Wedded Life* (Philadelphia: Presbyterian Board of Publication, 1886), p. 12.

15 Ibid., p. 10.

16 Jack Nelson, "Bush, Quayle Renominated; President Lauded as a Battler," *Los Angeles Times* (August 20, 1992): A9.

17 Nelson, p. 59.

18 Kahn, p. 3.

19 Nelson, p. 87.

20 Ibid., p. 71.

21 When one marries one obligates oneself, by a presumed choice to marry, to fulfill certain duties to one's family. On the other hand, one is born into obligation to a

biological family, with commensurate duties one is obliged to fulfill.

22 Nelson, p. 130.

23 Barrett and McIntosh, p. 77.

24 Even within heterosexual families, which conform to the presumed norm or ideal of family, questions of boundaries and identity emerge.

25 Adrienne Rich, "Compulsory Heterosexuality and Lesbian Existence," in Elizabeth Abel and Emily K. Abel, eds., *The Signs Reader: Women, Gender & Scholarship* (Chicago: The University of Chicago Press, 1983), pp. 139-168.

26 Ibid., p. 145.

27 According to The Oxford Universal Dictionary this comes from the Old English word "wed" - "A pledge, something deposited as security for a payment or the fulfillment of an obligation; occasionally, a hostage." and the word "lock" - "To close, enclose; a barrier, an enclosure."

28 Rich, p. 156.

29 Rosemarie Tong, *Women, Sex, and the Law* (Maryland: Rowman & Littlefield Publishers, Inc., 1984), p. 124.

30 Okin, p. 123.

31 Ibid., pp. 129-131.

32 Sarah Lucia Hoagland, *Lesbian Ethics: Toward a New Value* (Palo Alto, CA: Institute of Lesbian Studies, 1988), p. 29.

33 Ibid., p. 24.

34 Marian Wright Edelman, "Kids First!," *Mother Jones* (May/June 1991): 31-32 and 76-77.

35 Okin, p. 160.

36 Ibid., p. 166.

37 *U. S. Statistical Abstracts*, p. 51.

38 Weston, p. 187.

39 Paula Fomby, "Why I'm Glad I Grew Up in a Gay Family," *Mother Jones* (May/June 1991): 39.

40 Weston, p. 192.

41 Ibid., p. 44.

42 Hoagland, p. 54n.

43 Ibid., pp. 158-159.

44 Ibid., p. 75.

45 Ibid., p. 86. Similar understandings of this notion of sacrifice can also be found in the work of James Cone, Delores Williams, Beverly Wildung Harrison, and other liberationist writers.

46 Interview with Stone Philips on *Dateline* (11 August 1992), NBC.

47 Weston, p. 44.

48 Robert A. Johnson, *SHE: Understanding Feminine Psychology* (New York: Harper and Row, Publishers, 1976), p. 11. Johnson analyzes the myth of Amor and Psyche as a key to understanding feminine psychology. He notes that "Funeral rites and abduction ceremonies are still present in our weddings ... many a bride cries on her wedding day. Instinctively she knows that the maiden in her is dying."

49 Lindsey, p. 404.

50 As noted by U.S. Attorney General William French Smith in 1983. *TIME* (September 5, 1983).

51 Ruth Peachey, "National Estimates and Facts About Domestic Violence," *National Clearinghouse for the Defense of Battered Women,* 1988.

52 Lindsey, p. 400.

53 Weston, p. 25.

54 Beverly Wildung Harrison, "The Older Person's Worth in the Eyes of Society," in Beverly Wildung Harrison and Carol S. Robb, eds., *Making the Connections: Essays in Feminist Social Ethics* (Boston: Beacon Press, 1985), pp. 152-166.

55 Okin, esp. chapters 6 and 7.

56 Okin, pp. 126-127.

57 Harrison, p. 161.

58 Jim Cotter, "The Gay Challenge to Traditional Notions of Human Sexuality," in Malcolm Macourt, ed., *Towards a Theology of Gay Liberation* (London: SCM Press, 1977), p. 71.

59 Julie Ainslie and Kathryn M. Feltey, "Definitions and Dynamics of Motherhood and Families in Lesbian Communities," *Marriage and Family Review* 17.1/2 (1991): 63-85.

60 Carol Stack, *All Our Kin: Strategies for Survival in a Black Community* (New York: Harper and Row, 1974).

61 Elizabeth A. Say, *Evidence on Her Own Behalf: Women's Narrative as Theological Voice* (Maryland: Rowman and Littlefield Publishers, Inc., 1990), p. 100. This observation is part of a larger discussion of the work of Dorothy L. Sayers and her treatment of divine creativity.

62 Beverly Wildung Harrison, "Misogyny and Homophobia: The Unexplored Connections," *Making the Connections,* pp. 149-150.

63 We are indebted to Sharon Welch's concept of "communities of resistance and solidarity" in this regard.

64 Rita Nakashima Brock, *Journeys by Heart: A Christology of Erotic Power* (New York: Crossroad, 1988), p. 40.

65 Ibid., p. 35.

Notes on Contributors and Editors

J. Michael Clark, Ph.D. (Emory University,1980), is currently co-chair of the Gay Men's Issues in Religion Group of the American Academy of Religion and is both an "independent scholar" and a part-time instructor in the Freshman English Program of Georgia State University (Atlanta). Among his numerous publications are *Theologizing Gay: Fragments of Liberation Activity* (Oak Cliff, TX: Minuteman Press, 1991) and *AIDS, God, & Faith.* (Las Colinas, TX: Monument Press, 1992), co-written with Ronald E. Long. His most recent publication is *Beyond Our Ghettos: Gay Theology in Ecological Perspective* (Cleveland, OH: The Pilgrim Press, 1993).

Roger J. Corless, Ph.D. (University of Wisconsin-Madison, 1973), is an associate professor of religion at Duke University where he teaches history of religion and Chinese and Japanese Buddhism. He has written over forty articles on Buddhism, Christianity, and Buddhist–Christian Studies. His most recent publication is a review article of *The Eliade Guide to World Religions* by Mircea Eliade and Ioan P. Couliano with Hillary S. Wiesner (HarperCollins, 1991) and *Essential Sacred Writings from Around the World* by Mircea Eliade (Harper-Collins, 1991, re-issue of *From Primitives to Zen*, Harper and Row, 1967), which appeared in *Religion* 23 (1993): 373-377.

Richard P. Hardy, D. ès Sc. Rel. (Université de Strasbourg, France, 1967), is a professor of Christian spirituality at Saint Paul University in Ottawa, Canada. He has lectured in the area of Christian mysticism and spirituality in Hong Kong, Taiwan, and the Philippines as well as in the United States and Canada. He is the author of *Search for Nothing: The Life of St. John of the Cross* (New York: Crossroad, 1982), as well as several articles and other books on Christian spirituality published in Canada, the United States, the Philippines, and Taiwan. He is the co-ordinator for a special issue of *Église et théologie* (Ottawa) on "AIDS and Faith."

Susan E. Henking, Ph.D. (University of Chicago, 1988), is an assistant professor of religion at Hobart and William Smith Colleges in Geneva, NY. Her major teaching areas are religion and psychology, women's studies, and religion and the social sciences. She currently co-teaches a course on AIDS with one of her colleagues from the chemistry department.

Carter Heyward, Ph.D. (Union Theological Seminary, New York, 1980), is an Episcopal Priest and a professor of theology at Episcopal Divinity School in Cambridge, MA. She is the author of several books including *Touching Our Strength: The Erotic as Power and the Love of God* (San Francisco: Harper & Row, 1989).

Mary E. Hunt, Ph.D. (Graduate Theological Union, Berkeley, CA, 1980), is co-founder and co-director of the *Women's Alliance for Theology, Ethics, and Ritual (WATER)* in Silver Spring, MD. She has lectured throughout the United States, Europe, and Australia. Her most recent publication is *Fierce Tenderness: A Feminist Theology of Friendship* (New York: Crossroad, 1992).

Mark R. Kowalewski, Ph.D. (University of Southern California, 1990), has published articles on Gay men and AIDS, as well as on religious responses to the AIDS health crisis. After completion of his dissertation he worked as a post-doctoral research scholar with the Drug Abuse Research Group of the University of California, Los Angeles. He taught religion and social sciences in the Theology Department of Xavier University, New Orleans, before returning in 1992 to his former position as researcher with the Drug Abuse Research Group at UCLA.

Ronald E. Long, Ph.D. (Columbia University, 1985), is an adjunct professor in the Program in Religion, Hunter College/CUNY. He has taught at Columbia University and at Vassar College. He received his undergraduate education at Kenyon College and was a Fulbright scholar in Germany. His research interests focus on issues of fundamental theology in the light of the problem of natural evil and on issues surrounding the relation of religion and the erotic in Gay experience. Together with J. Michael Clark he wrote *AIDS, God, & Faith* (Las Colinas, TX: Monument Press, 1992), and is currently working on a study tentatively entitled *Remembering the Body.*

Elizabeth A. Say, Ph.D. (University of Southern California, 1988), is an associate professor in the Department of Religious Studies at California State University, Northridge. She researches and teaches in the areas of women and religion, ethics, and contemporary religious thought. Current research projects include the development of a feminist hermeneutic for narrative interpretation and she continues her work with Mark R. Kowalewski on a Lesbian/Gay critique and reconstruction of concepts of family. She has published *Evidence in Her Own Behalf: Women's Narrative as Theological Voice* (Savage, MD: Rowman & Littlefield Publishers, Inc., 1990).

Daniel T. Spencer, Ph.D. (Union Theological Seminary, New York, 1994), is an assistant professor of religion at Drake University, Des Moines, IA. At UTS he was a student of Beverly Wildung Harrison and Larry Rasmussen. He also worked with James Cone and specializes in questions regarding ecclesiology, ethics, and marginalized social groups.

Michael L. Stemmeler, Ph.D. (Temple University, 1990), is currently co-chair of the Gay Men's Issues in Religion Group of the American Academy of Religion and an assistant professor of religion at Central Michigan University. As leading co-editor of this series, he is the author of "Gays—A Threat to Society? Social Policy in Nazi Germany and the Aftermath" in *Homophobia & the Judaeo-Christian Tradition* (series volume 1; Dallas, TX: Monument Press, 1990) and "The Testing Game: HIV-Antibody Testing as Exercise of Socio-Political Power" in *Gay Affirmative Ethics* (series volume 4; Las Colinas, TX: Monument Press, 1993). He has co-produced a video on the experience of Gay life and homophobia on the college campus, *In Our Own Words: Lesbian, Gay and Bisexual Students at CMU* (Mt. Pleasant, MI: CMU-A/V Productions, 1992). He is the author of several papers on medical ethics and AIDS, and is currently working in the areas of Gay spiritual identity formation and the values of non-traditional relationships.